MATLEISURE

MATERNITY LEAVE SURVIVAL GUIDE
& THE ART OF ENJOYING IT

Emily Malloy

Matleisure
Copyright © 2023 by Emily Malloy

All rights reserved. No part of this publication may be reproduced, distributed, or transmitted in any form or by any means, including photocopying, recording, or other electronic or mechanical methods, without the prior written permission of the author, except in the case of brief quotations embodied in critical reviews and certain other non-commercial uses permitted by copyright law.

ISBN
978-0-2288-1136-7 (Hardcover)
978-0-2288-1137-4 (Paperback)
978-0-2288-1135-0 (eBook)

*To my mother, for teaching me what love is,
and my children, for shaping my understanding of life.*

Wherever you go, go with all your heart.

Confucius

CONTENTS

Foreword 1

Preface 3

Introduction 7

Chapter 1   Before Baby 11

Chapter 2   Postpartum 21

Chapter 3   Community 35

Chapter 4   Well-Being 47

Chapter 5   Connection 69

Chapter 6   Nourishment 83

Chapter 7   Movement 107

Chapter 8   Rest 113

Chapter 9   Apparel 129

Chapter 10   Finance 137

Chapter 11   Work 149

Chapter 12   Bonus 157

Conclusion 173

About The Author 175

FOREWORD

Being a mother? The best. Emily becoming a mother? A miracle and a mystery.

Emily is my daughter. She was a great kid. Curious. Friendly. "C'est un ange" was how her teachers described her—"She's an angel." The kind of kid you were proud to introduce to your friends. As an adult, she is extremely successful in the business world.

And now, Emily has written a book about early motherhood. She writes about the deep bond, the rhythm between a mother and her baby. She focuses specifically on maternity leave and goes into great detail about what it's like to be a new mother. Emily uses the knowledge and insight earned from her own experience and provides useful tools new mothers will find helpful.

MATLEISURE

This is a book about a big struggle, a big love. A book about wrapping your arms around a totally different life. A life so rewarding, so rich, so fulfilling that you fall to your knees in awe. This book will comfort all new mothers that happen upon it.

Emily thinks about things. About the meaning of all the stuff that happens around her. She knows what it's like to have a baby. The challenges that new mothers face and the intense joy. The effect of sleep-deprived nights, the smiles, the feel of a baby. In this book, Emily shares the solutions she came up with for how to handle the tough side of caring for a baby. You will also find solid, practical advice about the complex feelings of a new mother.

With a strong, friendly, compassionate voice, Emily guides you through the many stumbling blocks of early motherhood. She talks about how important it is for new mothers to feel good about themselves. It will feel as though she's right there with you. The love, the closeness, the wonder of it all will be yours when you open this book.

Jeannine Malloy

PREFACE

Typically, when faced with something new in my life, I turn to books for insight—something I learned from my mother. Reading about the experiences of others provokes thought in me, helps me understand how to embark on my own journey, and ultimately serves to develop my own wisdom. It opens my mind and enables me to consider various perspectives as I form my own ideas on the topic. Sometimes the usefulness of the information that I ingest only surfaces later. What I need in that moment is the comfort of knowing I'm not alone. Other times, I come across something that instantly resonates with me and allows me to gain so much clarity.

There are a ton of books on the topic of parenting, babies, and fertility. Some of which have had a profound impact not only on myself but also those around me. I'm so grateful to those that did take time to share their knowledge, because in some cases, it resulted in a significant shift in my perspective. But when it came down to the topic of maternity leave, I had a hard time finding a resource that really encapsulated the experience of early motherhood.

I took my first maternity leave with my daughter, Clementine Rose. In the months after her birth, I felt a wide range of raw emotions. It's like my heart literally expanded and left me more vulnerable than ever before. There were times when I was very uncomfortable and lost my sense of self. The people that were close to me were my lifelines. It took me a while to get the hang of things in the beginning.

Over the course of that first maternity leave, I learned things very gradually, through my own experiences and the community of mamas that I was lucky to be a part of. At some point, while I was in the thick of it all, I started documenting some of the things that made my life easier. Partly, I think, because I was sleep deprived and feared that I may forget, but also because I had this urge to write them down, with the hopes of eventually sharing my ideas with others that might find them useful.

Two years later, I had my second child, Spencer Wolf. My second maternity leave was vastly different. I applied a lot of the wisdom I'd gained from my first maternity leave and

PREFACE

learned a bunch of new things too. I realized the important role that your mindset plays in shaping your experience. I was notably calmer and able to enjoy some of more subtle delights that come with caring for a newborn. Most importantly, I leaned into the messiness of life for the first time, instead of running from it or hiding it from the world. Don't get me wrong, there were still a lot of challenges, but somehow, I was less afraid of doing what felt right for me.

This book sums up all things relating to maternity leave that were helpful to me, along with my thoughts on how to make your own leave enjoyable, in whatever way makes sense for you. I've added some of my experiences relating to these suggestions and as context for the advice I give, which I hope will be entertaining, if not helpful. The idea being that even in the most difficult times, when you likely won't feel like yourself, there can still be glimmers of light, things to have a chuckle about, and, perhaps most importantly, to inspire a little hope.

A few things to consider before you read on. Your first months of being at home with a new baby are meant to be a unique foray into parenthood, and ultimately, you'll define your own path. These are just a few ideas from my personal journey. Rest assured, it may sometimes appear that we live in an era of homogenized motherhood, but it's far from it.

MATLEISURE

Never have we been freer to pursue our definition of what it means to be a mother. I'm not saying that makes it an easy thing to do. But if at least one thing from my own enlightenment resonates with you and therefore improves your well-being as a new mama, it will have been worthwhile to share.

INTRODUCTION

This book is designed to be a reference, a type of survival handbook to help you make the most of your maternity leave. There's no one correct way to absorb the content in the pages that follow. You can read the book cover to cover in one go or you can opt to read the specific sections that are of most interest to you based on your needs. It's up to you! I've organized the topics and advice to make it easy to find again if you need to refer to it later when it's most useful. I have included all the tools that I have relied on to navigate the many bumps along the way. Some I had to put effort into, some were intuitive, and others I just stumbled on by chance.

One thing I know beyond a doubt is that life with a new baby is marked by this wonderfully turbulent and intensely chaotic time that is often scary, and during certain phases, incredibly hard. You will experience a whole range of new feelings. It's impossible to know how to do all the new things required and get it right every time.

You may never remember those first few weeks after the birth of your baby because you were in survival mode, and that's okay. There will be plenty of memories and special moments that you'll experience when you've come back to life.

Try to be as present as you can. Or else, it could feel like you're living in an endless loop of feeds, burps, and naps. Because you'll experience so many new things, it's easy to get lost in the shuffle and forget how truly amazing it is that you're alive (I'm being serious). It's important to be in the moment and take it all in, breathe, and not always be thinking five hundred steps into the future.

Don't try to be a hero. Go easy on yourself when things don't go as planned, and don't be afraid to ask for help when you need it. Always trust your instincts. Balance your own needs with the needs of your baby. Know that in the future, when you look back at your experience as a new mom, you'll be proud of yourself and what you have accomplished.

If you have a partner, I strongly encourage you to read or discuss each chapter together. I can guarantee that your

INTRODUCTION

bond as a co-parent will be tested. This book can be used as a neutral source to introduce ideas that can be talked through. No matter what kind of relationship you have with your partner, thinking about the new aspects of parenthood that will be covered in this book and keeping clear lines of communication open will undoubtedly be of great benefit to both of you. Actually, I'll go one step further and include a message directed at your partner below. Please have them read it!

Oh hello, you! You may not be the one physically giving birth or away from work yourself, and therefore not everything in this book will apply to you specifically. However, there's still a great deal of practical advice that you can apply during the maternity leave of your partner. You might also benefit from reading the advice as a way of thinking about the challenges that a new mother encounters during maternity leave, which can make the individual experiences feel shared between you and your partner. Trust me when I say that you'll be thrust into situations that go beyond your wildest imagination, and it'll be useful to have some guidance on how to weather them with more ease and support.

1

BEFORE BABY

First off, you're expecting? Wonderful news. This section will include some tips that you can easily check off while preparing for the arrival of a baby, a whimsical idea to consider, and hopefully some things to contemplate that were not even on your radar yet. If you read this entire book before you give birth, some things might not make sense and might even seem borderline silly. But trust me, there's no way you can truly fathom how the small details, like a green light versus a red light when you have a sleeping baby in the car, can literally make or break your whole day.

You may very well reach new levels on the spectrum of desperation that you didn't even know existed when it comes to the most basic things like sleeping, eating, showering, and time alone. After all, it's hard to fully comprehend how holding a baby for several continuous hours can really restrict your movements until you experience it.

Stock up on essentials

The spontaneous freedom that you used to have when it came to jetting out the door to run an errand on a moment's notice won't ever be quite the same. At least, not in the short term. You'll likely experience the biggest adjustment right after the birth of your baby, depending of course on your recovery needs. You might not even want to venture outdoors for other reasons.

Without going overboard (unless that's your thing, then by all means), it's nice to stock up on a variety of your favorite foods, dry goods, snacks, and other things that you like. Especially the ones that are harder to find. The same goes for household essentials like paper towels, toilet paper, detergents, and soap. Your favorite ice cream is a must-have!

Focus on the basics

For all baby-related gear, I would say get the big stuff that you absolutely need, like a car seat, crib, bassinet, stroller, bouncer, glider, changing station, feeding pillow, baby carrier, etc. It's important to unbox and test out the gear before the baby arrives to make sure everything is working well and nothing is missing from the box. If you have a car seat, doing a test run is recommended. Usually, these things are intuitive, but the last thing you want is to be figuring this out with a newborn in tow.

For the rest of the gear you'll eventually need, chances are that what you'll want will change over time as you develop your own preferences and learn about the unique likes and needs of your baby. These things are hard to predict in advance, so you can delay buying these items until later to avoid having a bunch of expensive, unused gadgets lying around the house, taking up valuable space.

Other baby necessities

It's a good idea to stock up on a few key items, like a week's worth of onesies and pajamas in newborn size and 0–3 months. Although, full disclosure, many babies skip newborn size altogether, so keep that in mind if you're buying lots of clothes ahead of time. Go for 100% cotton wherever possible, or other breathable, soft materials, and have them all washed and ready for use several weeks before your due date.

You might be drawn to the look of certain clothes, only to realize how impractical they are after the baby is born and never end up using them. As cute as newborn shoes are, I can pretty much guarantee that every family ends up with at least one pair that was never worn. Time flies during the newborn stage.

If you're going to introduce a lovey at some point (a comfort object for your baby), buy three identical ones that you can rotate. This will come in handy on the day you lose one, which will happen. Muslin blankets are great, lightweight and breathable, and can serve many purposes: blanket, swaddle, burp cloth, feeding cover. When it comes to diapers, it's practical to stock up, but it can be hard to predict how quickly your baby will outgrow each size, so keep that in mind.

Pack a hospital bag

This is basically a bag that has a few essentials to make your hospital stay more comfortable. Usually, you should aim to have it ready by thirty-five weeks. You might only stay in the hospital for a day, but if you have an unexpected C-section, or if your baby needs any additional care, your stay could be longer. It's a good idea to have a hospital bag even if you're planning a home birth because you never know if you'll end up in the hospital.

There are tons of resources online to get ideas on what to pack. My suggestion is to keep it simple: cell phone charger, socks, robe or loose clothing, maternity bras and underwear, toiletries, something to read, and some non-perishable snacks. And for baby, pack a coming-home outfit and a blanket. Your partner could also pack a hospital bag with a few essentials if they're so inclined.

Pet plan

If you have any friends of the animal variety, it could be a good idea to plan for someone to be able to care for them in case you have a longer-than-anticipated stay at the hospital. It could be as simple as giving someone a house key with accessible, written instructions, just in case. That way, you have one less thing to worry about. You should also consider helping your pet prepare for the baby's arrival with gradual steps, especially if you intend to introduce new rules or plan to restrict access to certain areas. Eliminating some behaviors takes time and practice!

Do something special

It can be anything from taking a babymoon—a vacation that you take with your partner before the baby is born—a weekend getaway, spending an evening with friends, a maternity photoshoot, or even just a prenatal massage. Think of something that would feel special that you can do alone or with your partner to celebrate the baby before it arrives. It doesn't have to cost money either. It can be as simple as jotting down your thoughts in a journal that you can share with your child at a later date.

Future childcare needs

Now is the time to think about your potential future childcare needs and start planning accordingly. Many people wait until the baby is born to get their name on a waitlist for childcare, but that's often too late, even if you're one year in advance of when you'll need childcare to start. In some areas, it can take up to two or three years to get a spot in your preferred childcare center. Many people end up having to make alternative arrangements to fill a childcare gap or opt for a solution that isn't ideal.

When considering childcare, small details like the proximity of the center to your home can make a big difference, especially when your baby is building up their immune system and may be sent home regularly for illness.

Your preference for childcare needs may change over time, and you may consider other avenues, like a family member or a nanny-share, but it's still advisable to keep your options open so you're not faced with the difficult situation of not having childcare when you need it. Take it from me, who had to do fifteen daycare tours while lugging around a newborn as a prerequisite to get on a waitlist, and in the end, none of them panned out in time.

Mini bucket list

I'm not talking about major life goals that you want to accomplish. Just make a list of all the things that you feel like you never have time to do, or things that you would like to do one day, for yourself or as a family.

It's important to take the time to do this gradually before the baby is born, slowly adding things so you don't feel rushed, while you have time to really think about it without putting too much pressure on yourself. Later, as your child grows up, it can be a handy reference tool when you're looking for inspiration.

Full disclosure, it may take months or years until you feel ready to consult this list—and don't be surprised to discover how much your priorities might have changed. There's something quite fascinating about tapping into your pre-baby mindset and perhaps finding a way to channel it.

If you have no idea where to start, try thinking about these categories: things to do, things to see, things to feel, and things to be thankful for.

Discuss important things

If you have a partner, I cannot stress how valuable it'll be to spend some time talking about parenthood with them before the baby is born. This is not meant to overwhelm you, as there are plenty of things that need to be addressed, and pregnancy sometimes goes by faster than you would expect.

It's important to make space to better understand your parenting values and expectations for each other. This will no doubt be an evolving conversation as the baby grows up and you face different challenges, but it's a real opportunity to be more prepared for some of the curveballs ahead.

For example, have a conversation around mental health, and perhaps aligning on what steps to take if your partner sees you overwhelmed and struggling. Or simply discuss different parenting roles that you might play. You can decide ahead of time if one parent could be responsible for bath time. It's a small thing that can hit two birds with one stone: it allows you to have a break and is a chance for your partner to regularly have their own special bonding session with the baby.

Future baby visitors

I recommend giving some thought now to how you want to handle and manage family and friends who'll want to visit the baby. After all, some people would opt to be in the delivery room if they could, but it's up to you and your partner to determine what you're comfortable with. Are you okay with people coming to the hospital or visiting you during those first few days at home?

Sometimes family members make surprise travels plans, which can be overwhelming to new mothers, so feel free to communicate your position on this in advance if you're worried it might happen. Parents often come for extended visits to help with the baby in the first few weeks, especially if they live out of town. It can be amazing to have an extra set of hands, but the visit can also come with a whole other set of mixed feelings depending on the preexisting dynamic you have with your visitors. If you do have someone staying with you, remember that the more clearly you communicate your needs, the smoother the visit is likely to go. Though, I know that can be hard at times.

You may very well not have the same comfort level and expectations as your partner and each of your families. I urge you not to feel pressured to entertain others during this time if you're not up for it. And if you do allow them, try to limit visits to short amounts of time, at least at the beginning. After all, you'll be in recovery mode, experiencing significant hormonal changes, and this is a very special and intimate time with your newborn. Either way, do what feels right for you, and don't be too hard on yourself. And try your best to align with your partner and share your preferences with your families and friends before the baby arrives.

2

POSTPARTUM

The first few days after childbirth are certainly not the perpetual state of bliss often depicted in mainstream media. It will likely be a mixture of all sorts of emotions and physical effects, and this is completely normal when you've been through a big life event, especially if you had a difficult delivery or unexpected complications during the birth of your child.

If at any time during the postpartum period, something doesn't feel right, trust your instincts and talk to your healthcare provider immediately. You are your best advocate, and this is not the time to be a people pleaser.

Beyond the post-birth logistics and other important things to be aware of and watch out for, in this chapter, I've also included several thoughts on how your current and future mindset will evolve and possibly be challenged in ways you never could've imagined.

Recovery needs

Postpartum recovery involves both your physical and mental health. Postpartum bleeding typically lasts up to six weeks. Outside of the physical recovery, which can include soreness, backaches, and healing from perineal tears, childbirth can also trigger mood swings and changes in hormones, which can manifest in unexpected areas, such as in your skin and hair. Every new mom is different and therefore will experience different postpartum symptoms. Although there are typically significant improvements after the six-to-eight-week mark, it can take much longer to feel like yourself again. Recovering from pregnancy and childbirth can take a long time.

If you end up having a C-section, and therefore had surgery, you must be extra careful during the healing process. It's important to follow the instructions from your healthcare provider, including the use of any pain medications if you're breastfeeding. Extra rest is always a good idea, but I can appreciate that this is not always possible, given the circumstances. After my C-section, I found it helpful to stock up on what I needed on different floors to avoid stairs in the early days. My best advice is to take it easy but not *too* easy. As in, don't wait longer than recommended to start doing gentle walks, because that can slow down the recovery process. I have heard that abdominal wraps can help but haven't tried them myself.

It's very common for women to experience pelvic floor disorders after having a baby, whether you've had a C-section or vaginal delivery. Pregnancy and birth can have a huge effect on your body, and it's normal that you may require some rehabilitation, especially if you're feeling pain or abdominal weakness, or experiencing incontinence. Most symptoms can be managed with therapy, but some may require surgery.

Whatever you do, don't be fooled into thinking that this is something you must accept as a consequence of childbirth. Even if you're not experiencing any immediate concerns in your recovery, consider seeing a pelvic floor therapist to preempt possible long-term issues.

In some countries, such as France, pelvic therapy is a standard part of the postpartum recovery process and is subsidized by the government! Here's to hoping more countries will adopt this practice, but in the meantime, it's important to advocate for yourself.

Feeding the baby

There's no right or wrong choice here, just the healthiest choice for you and your baby. And only you can know what that is, whether it's breastfeeding or bottle feeding. While breastfeeding is free and full of nutrients, it can also come with challenges. It's not easy for everyone to do successfully and may require hiring a lactation consultant to help (which is well worth it). Newborns eat quite frequently, so as the mother, you'll need to be available around the clock for constant breastfeeding, which can be very taxing, both physically and mentally.

As your milk regulates to align to your baby's needs, you may experience breast engorgement when your breasts have too much milk, and this can be very painful. Redness, pain, and swelling of the breasts, especially if you're warm or have a fever, could be a sign of mastitis and may require antibiotics.

In some ways, bottle feeding offers more flexibility, but if you're using breastmilk in the bottle, you'll need to pump milk several times a day. However, your partner or a family member can participate in the feeding when you need to rest or can't be there yourself. If you're feeding with formula, there are additional costs to consider and potential shortages of certain brands, due to supply chain issues. Formula does, however, offer the most flexibility out of all the options.

You don't have to have it figured out from day one. You can start by trying to breastfeed, and if that doesn't work out, switch feeding methods down the road. I recognize that this is easier said than done, as there can be some self-disappointment that comes with the inability to produce enough milk, or pressure from family to breastfeed. But try not to be too critical of yourself. Instead, feel empowered that you're making the right choice for your health and your baby's health.

If you need help or support with regards to feeding, speak to your healthcare provider, who can connect you to resources available in your area. Fed is best, no matter the method.

A tip for dry hands

You'll be washing your hands a lot during this period, as it helps to protect the baby's developing immune system. If you notice the skin on your hands beginning to get dry, try to get it under control before it gets very bad. If you're not careful, your knuckles can crack and begin to bleed, and this can be very painful. The healing process is much longer when it gets to this stage. Pure shea butter worked best to soothe my hands when nothing else was helping.

Checkups & appointments

Usually there's a scheduled checkup with your healthcare provider around the six-week mark to give you the all clear to resume certain activities. In some areas, guidance has been revised to include an initial assessment within the first three weeks following childbirth, which is great news. There will also be regular check-ins for your baby to ensure that they're growing, feeding, and developing as they should be. The appointments are a good opportunity to ask any questions that you may have.

Sometimes getting to these appointments can be quite challenging, especially if you're still recovering. You might get advice that is contradictory, like being told that you cannot drive or lift anything heavier than your baby while also being expected to bring the baby to appointments that require use of a car and heavy car seat. Ask for clarity whenever you need it, and be open about your personal circumstances so that you're not feeling confused as to the best course of action. If you need special accommodations for pumping or feeding while at any of your appointments, don't be afraid to ask about what your options are.

On the days when you've had little sleep, making it to the doctor's office and back is an accomplishment in its own. Remember that.

Getting support

I know that asking for help isn't always an easy thing to do. Chances are, the people around you would like to support you during this time, especially if they're related to the baby. If someone asks you what you need, requesting meals is a great way to ease into welcoming help from others. Things like precooked dinners that can easily be reheated, casseroles, or food delivery services can really help in the first few weeks after the baby is born.

And if you don't have people lining up to help you, I encourage you to ask for it. People in your entourage might not understand what you're going through, especially if you're the first in your friend group to have a baby. Vocalizing your needs might be difficult at first, but I've found that when you have a baby, the world becomes a friendlier place. If you're open to it, strangers even go out of their way to assist you.

Postpartum depression (PPD) & psychosis (PPP)

Moods swings and a roller coaster of emotions, sometimes called "baby blues," are quite typical in the first few weeks after childbirth, but they usually subside over time with rest and time for yourself. If for whatever reason you're still feeling overwhelmed several weeks after birth, and you're experiencing depression symptoms, it's possible that you may have developed postpartum depression, and it's important to seek medical help to get support.

Male postpartum depression, sometimes also known as paternal postnatal depression (PPND), also exists and can be present during the first few years of fatherhood.

Remember that this is a very stressful and exhausting period, and postpartum depression can make it even more difficult. It's nothing to be ashamed or embarrassed about, and it's not your fault. Postpartum depression is common, and if you speak to your healthcare provider (e.g., obstetrician, midwife, family doctor), they can evaluate your symptoms and create a treatment plan that will suit your needs and help you cope with everyday life with your new baby. You can also talk to a therapist about local support groups for new moms who are also experiencing postpartum depression. If you're in need of immediate support, I encourage you to reach out to a hotline right away for help.

Canada
Wellness Together
1-866-585-0445

POSTPARTUM

United States
National Maternal Mental Health
1-833-943-5746

Worldwide
Postpartum Support International
1-800-944-4773

A medical professional can help diagnose and treat postpartum depression as well as postpartum psychosis, which is a much rarer and more severe condition that can cause delusions or hallucinations and requires immediate emergency medical care.

Inner mama bear

Being a mama is like living in that house within the beautiful landscape in Western movies. At the beginning, you're just waiting for that first sign of danger, like the faint but increasing sound of galloping horses carrying dangerous cowboys coming over the mountain, coming to destroy everything you hold so dearly. And how could they not? You have in your possession the greatest treasure of all time, something that you must protect at all costs—your newborn.

This may sound a tad dramatic if you haven't had your baby yet. But don't be fooled. This intensely protective feeling can easily sweep over you. It's something that just kicks in. I remember feeling ready to defend myself from anybody who even looked remotely suspicious as I was walking down the street with my baby, something that's quite out of character for me. Don't worry, the intensity of this mama bear feeling should subside over time, as your baby gets stronger and less helpless.

As intense as this uncomfortable feeling can be for those experiencing it, sometimes the absence of it can feel equally alarming. Not all mothers will experience this feeling, or it may come at a later time. In some cases, mothers suffering from postpartum depression feel a disconnect from their newborn and should take this as a sign to seek medical attention.

Changing standards

Regardless of how sure you are about your approach to parenting, it's likely that your perspective will change over time. Stay open to the evolution of your own ideas, because you'll be exposed to so many new and different situations. The idea is that we shouldn't hold too strongly to a belief that no longer serves us or doesn't suit our needs or our life circumstances anymore, and that it's okay to change ourselves with the changes around us.

The one constant during early motherhood is change. The more you can embrace it versus fighting it, the better position you'll be in to appreciate how you can learn from these changes and better enjoy all the early developmental stages of your baby. And if that means outgrowing your previous standards, so be it!

Lesser-of-two-evils state of mind

Basically, it's just a different way of looking at things. For example, pre-parenthood, if you saw a baby unraveling a whole toilet paper roll, you might think, "Why would a parent let them do that? It's causing a mess!" But when you're staring at your own baby doing this, you realize there's more to the story. Perhaps the unrolling of the toilet paper is distracting them from vigorously opening and closing all the bathroom drawers and potentially squishing little fingers. In that light, the toilet paper doesn't seem so bad. Choosing the lesser of two evils might happen naturally when you're faced with these types of scenarios many times a day. Embrace it if you can!

It's okay not to have all the answers

Say this out loud. And again. One more time, just for the road. Write it on a Post-it note while you're at it. This is about giving yourself permission to be okay with an increased level of unanswered questions at any given time, while making sure that you don't get overwhelmed by all the things you don't know, like future things you haven't decided on yet or don't need to figure out in the immediate term. It doesn't mean you can't think about it. Just make sure it's not dominating the present.

Meeting your worst self

This is exactly what it sounds like. It's a lot. It's intense. Your best self won't always be at the forefront. You may have a short fuse. You may be more volatile than you usually are, which frankly, is to be expected from someone who's likely hungry, tired, and possibly touched out—that feeling of being constantly touched and needing a break from physical contact.

This is a time when everybody is talking about all the blissfulness of being a new mother, which, of course, can be true in many ways. Getting to experience all the things that come with being around a newborn, like seeing them smile for the first time, is truly magical. But this is also happening at the same time as you're recovering from giving birth,

POSTPARTUM

having to learn a ton of new things. You have very little time to process everything that's happening around you, and you have this huge responsibility of keeping a tiny human alive.

If you happen to be very self-aware, you may notice you're not acting like yourself, and that's hard! Especially if you're feeling powerless in being able to change how you're showing up to your partner. Being faced with the worst version of yourself that you've ever been is pretty much unavoidable, but it's normal. Try to speak to your partner openly about your struggles and ask for some grace in those especially difficult moments. Gentle reminder—they are not mind readers.

Having an open and honest conversation about this with a close friend, someone who's already a mom and someone you trust, might be a good idea. While I wish there was a way to prevent this from happening, I hope that the knowledge that it's coming and that it's normal will be at least helpful in working through it.

And a reminder here that if you're feeling overwhelmed and are having difficulties taking care of the baby, you may be experiencing postpartum depression, and it's important to talk to your healthcare provider.

Learn to forgive yourself

Do me a favor and try to go easy on yourself. You won't always have all the right information to make all the best decisions all the time, and I can pretty much guarantee that you'll look back on a few things that you did and cringe. You'll think, I could have done better, here, there, and everywhere.

Nobody's keeping track of your perfect score as a mother. We're meant to make mistakes; we're also learning and doing things for the first time. We all know we can't change the past, and we only have some control over what happens in the future. But we do have full control over how we see things, past and present.

How will you decide to think about your own journey? What have you learned that you can bring with you into the future? Practicing forgiveness will also make it easier to extend to others. The more we do it, the more natural it becomes. And over time, the easier it'll become to identify with that feeling and forgive yourself.

3

COMMUNITY

I cannot stress how crucial it is to be a part of a community in early motherhood, because trust me, it's marvelous, and it's up to you to manifest it. Like dating, it's a question of chemistry. You don't know who you'll gel with. I can tell you there's tremendous comfort and solace in connecting with someone who's going through something similar to you in the moment you're faced with it, even if you don't think you need them right now. There's no such thing as too many online mom groups—okay, kidding.

Keeping an open mind toward connecting with new people or deepening your existing friendships can really strengthen your support network, which will serve to help you navigate the many trials and tribulations that await you (and join you in celebrating the big milestones). Sometimes it's just about having a safe space to vent, seeing a familiar face when attending local baby-geared activities in your community, or even just having someone to chat with when feeding your baby in the middle of the night.

Don't be too fussed if you can't find an exact replica of your vision for parenting style in your mama crews. You'll realize that even if you don't plan on giving battery-operated toys to your child, and perhaps you and your support mamas diverge in opinion on decisions like these, you can still find many things that draw you together.

In all seriousness, hitting rough patches are par for the course, and challenges like sleep deprivation bring all mamas together. Here are a few different types of relationships that I count myself lucky to have in my life, both online and in the real world. They're here to serve as inspiration to build your own community, along with a few of my other thoughts and ideas on the topic.

Existing mama friends

These are all your friends and acquaintances who became mamas before you. You likely didn't give them enough credit at the time. You were probably off gallivanting and being all carefree and didn't grasp the true miracle they were experiencing. They are the perfect mix of experienced peers and people who knew you before you became a mama. You'll finally understand why it was impossible to reach them at certain times. You can appreciate what they were going through from afar, but now, you have a newly acquired visceral understanding of what they experienced when they became a parent. This brings you closer.

But don't feel bad, the feeling was mutual! They were not necessarily gravitating towards your uninformed state either. Now you can connect on a whole new level and reignite your friendship if need be. Existing mama friends are also great because they can give you lots of perspective on what's to come.

Non-mama friends

A community wouldn't be complete without non-mama friends too. First of all, it's your duty to communicate all the wonderful joys of being a parent to them so you can trick them into becoming a parent too—I kid, I kid. But also, it's important to make an effort to keep in touch because you might not naturally run into them as frequently as before.

Being that they're not responsible for a tiny human being, they likely have more flexibility to come spend a weekend to visit you and work around your love-hate relationship with your baby's ever-evolving nap schedule. Yes, they may not be as enthusiastic about seemingly insignificant growth spurts that your baby is currently experiencing. However, they can give you a reality check, if you need it, from a non-parenting point of view. Plus, this may be your only chance to talk about something other than the baby. You get to live vicariously through them, even if it's just for a hot second.

In-the-trenches mamas

Picture yourself wearing the same ponytail for five days—the elastic is so low it's barely holding on. Even if you squint in the mirror, you can no longer mistake your look as an intentional bedhead mama vibe. You don't remember the last time you had a shower, you lost track of all the food, milk, and spit-up that's ended up on your shirt. In fact, when a new mystery stain pops up, you don't even bother investigating what it is.

You leave the house to run an errand, and you run into a fellow mama, but you don't feel embarrassed at all. You're just happy to see them. Their presence is like a warm hug. In the few minutes that you speak to each other, you feel energized and understood. No matter what you do or say, you never feel judged by these mamas. They understand how parenting can be a struggle because they're likely experiencing the same thing as you.

If you can't picture someone like this in your life now, it's okay. You might meet this person later during your mat leave. I have a few of them, and I love them dearly. They're someone I can text at any time of the day or night, and they'll say to me, "Emily, you got this." And I'll believe them. They're someone who'll never get upset at a last-minute cancellation of plans because life happens, and it'll never get in the way of your friendship and supporting each other.

Cultivating these types of relationships requires you to be vulnerable. That's a key factor. I know that's not easy, because there are so many expectations that we place on ourselves at any given time. But if you feel comfortable trusting someone with your true self (the good and bad), you stand to gain a very meaningful relationship, and that can be a tremendous support during this time.

Random mamas out in the world

Some of my closest friends are mamas that I met almost completely by chance. I had recently moved to a new city, so I didn't have a preexisting network of friends that I could tap into after the baby was born. So, I was very open to the idea of cultivating new connections, especially if they felt natural.

The thing with parenthood, in my experience anyway, is that it becomes okay again to approach strangers and have very personal conversations while you're just at the park hanging out. It reminded me of the dog park when you have a dog. Somehow, when you enter the little gated park, it becomes socially acceptable to have conversations with people you don't know who are just standing around.

If you're open to it and looking to form connections with other new moms, it'll take some practice, a little courage, and may require stepping out of your comfort zone, but it's so worth it! You have nothing to lose by trying. One idea: strike up a conversation with another new mom that you encounter while you're out and about with your baby. It can be while you're in line at a grocery store, or after mom and baby yoga class, or while browsing in a baby boutique.

The trick here is to try to avoid saying something that can make the other mom feel judged or giving unsolicited advice as an icebreaker, because that will likely backfire, and speaking from experience, it's easy to do so unintentionally without even thinking about it. If you do this by accident, show yourself some grace.

COMMUNITY

If you end up in a conversation that feels natural, as awkward as this might feel in the moment, try to find a way to stay connected after the initial interaction. If you don't want to give away your phone number, it can be as simple as connecting on social media. That way, you can continue to build on the connection and perhaps arrange a baby playdate at a later time.

Another way to connect is to be open to the interactions that come your way organically and turn them into connections. When I was in the last two weeks of my pregnancy, while at a nail salon, the woman sitting next to me was also a new mom and asked me about my pregnancy and how I was doing. She offered to add me to some local mom and baby groups on social media and shared other resources that were very valuable, and we exchanged contact information.

Unexpectedly, I gave birth the following day, so when she reached out to follow up, we ended up chatting and really clicked. Later, this same friend was selling a used maternity bra to another mom on a local group. They struck a conversation and ended up becoming fast friends. The three of us spent a large chunk of our maternity leaves together, and I am so grateful that our paths crossed, as they had a huge impact on my well-being and my early days of motherhood.

One final idea that you can consider is joining local mom groups, either through social media or through an app, and posting openly that you're looking to create and form new connections with other moms. You can suggest a weekly mom and baby drop-in playdate at a local park or on a walk. I see these types of posts often and so many responses from other moms looking to connect. I know it can feel daunting and perhaps overwhelming to put yourself out there, but remember that so many new moms are feeling just like you and looking for connection with other moms. If you prefer, you can search past postings to see if there are any standing meetups in your area.

Either way, if this is important to you, it's worth putting in the effort to find new connections. Not all of them will turn into deep, long-lasting relationships. The point is to have a community of others that can support and understand you if that's what you need in the moment. And equally important and worth considering is that if you're not feeling the connection with someone, don't feel obligated to continue the relationship.

Unicorn online mama group

What is a unicorn mama group you ask? What makes them so great? It's basically a diverse group of mamas who are all lovely and raw and genuine. A place where all mamas can ask for advice or rally behind another mama who is going through a tough phase with their little one. With a little patience, you'll find this magical community. It's a great resource to get information on baby products, to poll other mamas for what is reasonable in all these new situations you're facing, or even just to get a few words of encouragement. Some days, we just need to hear that we are doing a good job. Sometimes these groups are closed or hard to find, because you must be added to them by someone that knows you personally.

Creating your own community

If the type of mom group or community that you yearn for doesn't exist, consider creating it yourself. I've seen it done many times, and it's so amazing to watch a community of like-minded people grow into something meaningful. It doesn't have to be a large community; it can be any size and either open or closed to the public. You'll soon find others who wish to join.

It can be as simple as forming a social group with the people who were in your prenatal class. Chances are, your babies were born fairly close together, which means that staying in touch can give you a network of parents who are also going through the same baby milestones down the road.

You can also pool resources with your prenatal group to hire specialists or consultants and save money.

Another idea is creating an online community based on an area of interest. For example, a friend and I started a social media account to share simple and easy parenting hacks and recipes. It was a way for us to keep track of successes and find ways to connect with other moms.

Community for partners

In my experience, communities for partners are not as common. It may take a bit of effort to put one together, and they might require your help, but it's very much worthwhile from what I hear. If you live in a neighborhood with young families, you can do an outside get together to create opportunities to make connections. Or you can encourage your partner to create a group online. As I understand it, creating this space for your partner can uncover new avenues for emotional connection and bonding from a partner's perspective and take some pressure off your relationship as the sole source of connection.

A few watchouts

As amazing as communities can be, it's not all rosy out there. Online, there are usually guidelines for appropriate behavior (mutual respect, no hate speech or bullying, respecting privacy, adding trigger warnings, etc.). Admins moderate these forums to ensure the rules are followed, but they can't be everywhere at once. When asking for advice on a parenting forum, you may not appreciate some of the comments from others or feel hurt and judged.

It's important to remember that if a community is not benefitting you, you can leave if that's what best for you. Some people have very harsh opinions with regards to the best practices and standards of motherhood and are not afraid to share them. Things can quickly escalate, and it's easy to get swept up into highly emotional debates that can have a direct impact on your mental health. Proceed with caution, protect your energy when possible, and feel empowered to step away when necessary.

A note on isolation

There will be times when, no matter how much you know that you're loved, no matter how large your support community is, no matter how much you love your baby . . . you will feel alone and perhaps very disconnected from everything you once knew, including your personal relationships. To be fair, your whole world changed overnight. You're likely feeling a bunch of new things, both physical and emotional, and it may take some time to figure out how to make sense of it all.

MATLEISURE

If this is something you're struggling with, don't suffer in silence for too long. Try sharing this with someone that you're comfortable with, someone who knows you. Perhaps they have a few ideas that can be helpful. If the feelings persist over time, speak with your healthcare provider to get an assessment to determine if you need further support.

4

WELL-BEING

Mama-drenaline

/mama-əˈdren(ə)lən/

noun

A magical hormone secreted by the adrenal glands in mothers following the birth of a baby, characterized by increased stress, prolonged absence of continuous sleep, lack of time to shower or to do anything for oneself, irregular eating habits, and little-to-no exercise beyond lifting baby, resulting in semi-permanent frowning, inability to relax, greatly reduced emotional intelligence, and forgetfulness regarding non-baby-related things (AKA things that can wait).

Joking aside, what I refer to as mama-drenaline (even if technically speaking, I made up that definition) is this snowball effect of an adrenaline-like feeling which accumulated over the first few months of doing my best to keep my baby thriving.

Before I got pregnant, I was usually able to make space for my own needs in relation to those of others. After the baby was born, I was still somewhat able to recognize that I required some downtime to recharge, yet I had so many immediate and pressing responsibilities that always appeared more important than my own.

Here's the thing. One aspect of your life cannot overwhelm the rest. I get that you're a mother, but you were a person before you were a mother, and that person had needs. Do not ignore these needs! If you do not find a way to diffuse all this pent-up energy, it will take a toll on you in the long run.

I once volunteered to go pick up some driveway salt in the winter at night and thoroughly enjoyed the outing, which is quite indicative of my state of being at the time. Making time to invest in your own well-being will take effort. It must be deliberate and self-initiated and encompasses so much more than just doing something for yourself. It will enable you to start feeling like yourself again. Here are a few ideas of things to consider in this post-baby world where time alone is in many ways the new currency.

Practice self-care

Just to be clear, I don't consider things like going to the grocery store alone or having a nap when you've been up all night with the baby to be self-care. Those are just basic human needs. Self-care is supposed to give you new energy. It can be making time to connect with a friend, read a book, or just enjoy the company of an empty room for a little while.

Something that worked well for me was finding ways to reconnect with my senses. Prolonged lack of sleep would cause my facial muscles to tense up. One day during my shower, I stood facing the showerhead with the steady flow of water directly on my face for several minutes. Intense? Yes. But by golly, did I ever feel relaxed afterwards, and it became a regular part of my routine.

Daily evening baths also helped me tremendously, especially in the winter months. After a busy day of navigating cold winds, snow, and who knows what else, you just want your body to feel overwhelmed by warmth, even if just for a few minutes—and that last point is important. It only takes a few minutes to feel a big difference. Ten to fifteen minutes, and it's like you're a new person. I usually add Epsom salt (a lot, like one to two cups), baking soda (half cup), and a few drops of eucalyptus essence. The more baths you take, the more you'll love baths. They can become this great, relaxing ritual at the end of a long day.

Embrace your hair

Having a hairstyle that's easy to manage and makes you feel good is worth figuring out, as you might not have the same amount of time as you previously did to wash and style it. Keeping my hair long and having bangs made my life way simpler and less stressful. It's easy to put up in a ponytail, and bangs can be washed in the bathroom sink in a pinch to feel refreshed.

There's currently a whole wave of encouragement toward loving the natural hair that you have, instead of trying to manipulate it to no end, both when it comes to texture and form but also color. Being exposed to all sorts of people sharing their own experiences has really helped me. That's not to say that you can't change your hair or style it to suit your own preferences, but the point is that you should feel comfortable to do what's right for you and perhaps be open to trying something new.

Bring in some fresh air

Getting regular clean air in all the rooms of your home feels really nice. With a new baby, it's easy to spend hours cocooning and forget to air out your rooms to allow fresh air to come in. So go ahead and open the windows and doors for a few minutes to increase airflow and allow for circulation. Just don't leave them open for too long in the winter because this could impact your heating bill.

The power of music

I know I don't have to convince anyone on the science of why music is good for humans. What I will do, however, is offer a reminder that if you haven't listened to music in a while, maybe it's a good time to reintroduce it into your life. I know in my case, my life felt so shaken up for a little while there, it took some time for the dust to settle and for me to realize that I was missing out on something that gave me so much joy and helped me to feel relaxed. Also, it's a great time to discover new music, genres, and artists that will create new, vivid memories during this important time of your life.

Play!

No, seriously. Kids do it all the time, and I think maybe adults do too—although they may call it something else. In truth, it's less about what you're doing and more about the feeling. What gives you pleasure just because? It can be anything, really. Could be something you used to do as a child or in some way related to that, like music, sports, dancing, or making art.

Having fun, laughing deeply, or doing something without the need to be productive is so freeing. A release of sorts. Maybe it's only for five minutes to start, if time for play is hard to come by. I'm no stranger to the pull of Netflix whenever I have a few minutes to spare, so I can be transported to a new world and disconnect. That's totally acceptable, but it's also important to consider how you feel coming out of spending time doing that. What is your exit vibe like? Does it help to give you the energy needed to keep tackling the day, or do you feel even more depleted? Maybe a bit of both?

Next time you reach for your phone, make a list of all the things you used to do as a kid that you loved, and see if maybe it's possible to try to do one of them instead sometime when you're in the mood for something different.

Daylight sky gazing

Staring at the sky can give you a sense of calm by bringing you more awareness of the world around you. It's especially useful during those months with fewer daylight hours. It's easy to get so lost in your day that you forget to appreciate the natural wonders that are around us. Sunlight and sky are beautiful and have many benefits for us. Try it to see if skygazing can help you de-stress in difficult moments.

Practice gratitude

The benefits of feeling gratitude are rarely contested, but practically speaking, as a new mother, it can be challenging to even remember to feel gratitude in the first place, let alone regularly. When you're having a tough day and you know that you're teetering on the edge of unreasonableness (yes, that's a word), a moment of feeling grateful can be all you need to keep going. I try to practice gratefulness every day at twilight (which I have called *blue time* since I was a child), and it's usually a peaceful time of day. I also like it because it has a visual cue that helps to serve as a reminder no matter what I'm doing or where I am.

And while I'm on the topic, it's possible that for some of you, the notion of gratitude will be deeply intertwined with your worst fears. This was the case for me. In the first few months after my daughter was born, whenever I dared to think about how grateful I was for her, what immediately followed were thoughts about how afraid I was that one day she would die. These thoughts were so powerful and came right on the coattails of my purest thoughts of gratitude. It was like I couldn't separate these two opposing ideas, no matter how hard I tried.

I don't have a magical answer to how to deal with this, but it got better over time, in case that helps. From a general perspective, embracing the inherent vulnerability that becoming a parent has bestowed upon me, and overcoming my urge to fight it, has also been very beneficial.

Mindfulness

Don't worry if you're new to meditation and don't know where to start. A good way to get going is by doing a bit of research. There are plenty of apps, many of which are free, that offer guided meditations. There are also videos online that are short in length, which are perfect for beginners and can help you figure out what works best for you. Later in the book I share my favorite mediation app.

A lot of people claim they don't have time to meditate. I think that if you have time to breathe, you have time to meditate. It's a question of prioritizing, as meditating can have an exponential impact on your well-being and your personal relationships. We're always looking for that miracle food that is so nutritious and delicious and holds innumerable benefits to your body. I like to think of meditation as a superfood for your brain. It's free and worth every drop. I find that I'm in much better spirits and feel as though I can do anything when I meditate regularly.

Once in a blue moon, when I wake up before everybody else in the house, I spend thirty minutes meditating in bed, first thing in the morning. In a pinch, even when I only have time for a one-minute session, I'm still happy. I would often do very simple meditation exercises while breastfeeding.

Making this a daily habit helps you live in the moment with increased clarity and has a great calming effect. One of the first meditations that truly resonated with me was a guided exercise where you visualize yourself as a mountain—you're unwavering, grounded, and still experiencing lots of change on the surface. There are many videos of this meditation online if you want to give it a try!

The concept of self-grace

If you haven't already, you'll probably notice that I tend to remind you to be gentle on yourself in various circumstances throughout these pages. It's because I know how hard we can sometimes be on ourselves, even if we don't always like to admit it.

Try not to be overwhelmed by guilt, because it adds up over time and doesn't serve anybody any good. The concept of mommy guilt is pretty universal, and it arises from feeling like you're not meeting the expectations of what a perfect mother is supposed to be. You may guilt yourself for not accomplishing all the things you wanted to do, not spending enough time interacting with your baby, having a messy home, the list goes on. A little compassion toward yourself can go a long way.

Remember that your present circumstances do not allow you to have full control over your productivity because you're simultaneously caring for another human being. At the end of any given day, you may feel like you have nothing to show for it except a bigger pile of laundry, but that's nothing to feel badly about. After all, you kept your tiny human alive, and that's what matters.

Sometimes, it helps to reassess what these feelings of guilt are rooted in. So often, I have a negative thought and I must consciously re-evaluate if this idea is even realistic based on my current circumstances. Is it based on a belief that I have just accepted without question? We're always evolving as humans, in our relationships and in our ideas. And sometimes it's a good idea to pause and observe how we feel in the present. There's no right or wrong here, but it's important to make sure that you still feel connected to what is driving your behavior.

There are ways of incorporating the notion of self-grace within your daily life. For example, if you're looking to achieve a specific goal, you can set general expectations on the behaviors that you want to develop to achieve that goal, rather than framing it around a quantifiable output, as this opens the door to potential failure and shame when things don't go as initially planned (which is par for the course when you're caring for a baby). Framing your goals to do as much as you can on any given day can help keep you on task, even if you have a less productive day than expected during your maternity leave.

Make a "to-NOT-do" list

List making is somewhat of a balancing act. Ultimately, it's meant to be a tool to better prioritize energy and focus. But as we all know, if you add too many items to the list that are hard to achieve, it can be overwhelming and its very existence work against you.

Enter the concept of the "to-NOT-do" list. Why am I proposing a whole new listing strategy, you ask? Well, here's the thing. As a new mom, you have so many things coming at you in real time that it can become hard to process them and make sense of it all. You can sometimes get swept up in doing something, perhaps because of your entourage of other moms, social media, or whatever it may be. It's possible that it may take you a little longer to clue in that some of the things you're doing are either not worth your time, not working toward your goals, or not bringing you great pleasure.

Sometimes, you want to please people, so you might just agree to do stuff. And in the world of new motherhood, the number of things other people want you to do tends to multiply, like exponentially. From time to time, it's a good idea to reassess what is important to you as a family and make sure other less important things are not getting in the way.

Here's a tip to get started on your "to-NOT-do" list. Think about all the things that you did in the last couple of weeks (or further back, if you can recall), and for each activity or thing you did, ask yourself if you want to keep doing it, do it more, or eliminate it. In my experience, the simple act of taking the time to actively think about it and write it down can be very enlightening.

When in doubt, just tell yourself that you're an adult and you're in charge of your destiny. Remind yourself to be selective with your time. That's what I do. Nobody should ever feel forced to attend weekly song circles if it's not your jam—or your baby's jam, for that matter.

Quick delivery options

Explore options in your area for same-day delivery, whether it's for groceries, pharmacy stuff, diapers, pet food, etc., because at times, there'll be things that you will need badly, for which it'll be very convenient to be able to order at the click of a button. It's also possible in some regions to set up recurring weekly grocery deliveries. It's a great way to stay on top of weekly essentials needed with minimal effort. The only thing I would caution against is that this new ease of ordering online can encourage impulsive and sleep-deprived spending for some new mothers, so it's worth pre-planning and considering your purchases accordingly.

Habit mingling

New habits can be hard to introduce, let alone maintain. What has really helped me make time for healthy habits is to attach a particular habit to something else that happens on a regular basis. It's almost like creating a buddy system but for habits.

For example, flossing. On some days, taking time to floss in the morning felt like a luxury. I would easily go months without flossing because I simply felt that I could not make the time. I decided to floss at night during the baby's bathtime routine. By anchoring the habit of flossing to something else that happened almost every day, it helped me to take the focus away from feeling like I never had the time, until I was automatically reaching for the floss without even thinking about it.

Parent club

Call it whatever you want: book club, stamp club, wine club, adult club, trivia club, baby-poo-explosion-stained-shirt club. The idea is to leave the house with other parents, occasionally under the guise of a theme. Sounds simple enough, right? Wrong. This will take a lot of effort. I repeat, this will take a truckload full of effort. I have a few groups of amazing mama friends, and it takes us months to figure out the day and the location.

Even with careful planning, there's always a high probability that many will be no-shows because that's just life as a parent and the fact that babies (as they should) have no care in the world for your extracurricular activities. It's not like someone plans to get hand, foot, and mouth, right? But I cannot stress how important it is to strive for activities without your baby, and it's especially fun to hang out with the people you typically only see with baby in tow. Think about it, you can have a full conversation without interruption—it's truly divine!

Anyhow, I would say that if you plan for these on a semi-regular basis, you might pull off going to these once or twice a year, which in my opinion would be considered a success. And prepare yourself to be shocked at how fast time flies during these gatherings!

Final thought on the subject: on my way home after a fun night out, I would often be left with a feeling of melancholy, like the brief but definite emptiness that you experience when you finish reading an amazing novel (oh, just me? Never mind then). If you feel the same, don't worry. The feeling doesn't last forever.

Schedule solitude time

I firmly believe that your brain needs time to rest. Prior to having a baby, you likely had a lot more solo time, although you probably didn't fully appreciate it. Damn you, hindsight.

The idea of scheduling probably sounds a bit extreme, but the reality is that opportunities won't magically present themselves to you. And while occasionally, you may plan to take a night away from the baby, it probably won't be enough. I felt like I was always chasing time alone, so I realized I had to be more purposeful with my approach.

Instead of aiming for large stretches of time, try smaller, more achievable bouts of time that don't require as much coordination to make them happen. Whether it's predetermining them in advance on a shared calendar with your partner or finding childcare for a few hours, once the planning part is done, it's more straightforward to do it and feel the benefits. Which reminds me, some gyms have short-term daycare onsite. It's worth seeing what your local options are.

Reduce mental fatigue

When you're a new parent, there are a lot of decisions, big and small, that need to be made on any given day. It's important not to wear yourself out on all the small, mundane stuff, because, as a result, you'll have zero energy left to make other more important decisions which require more careful thought.

Habits are a great way to help protect mental energy, as it takes less energy to repeat established tasks than it does to continually create new ones. I found it very helpful to predetermine blocks of time every week to accomplish certain recurring tasks, like grocery shopping, laundry, and watering the plants (that were still alive).

Something else to consider is the concept of mono-tasking. Even if you defied the odds against multitasking successfully in your previous life sans kids, it'll be hard in your current state, as it's highly likely you're sleep-deprived. Don't expect a great batting average for multitasking with a newborn. So, instead of trying to do a million things at once and then getting discouraged because you're failing at them, try focusing on one thing at a time. Do it well. Allow yourself to concentrate on it, and do it with intent.

Realistically, if you're a hardwired multitasker to the bone (nice to meet you, friend), the joys of mono-tasking might seem like a stretch. I'm not suggesting you completely shift to the other side of the tasking spectrum. But if (or when) you start burning food in the kitchen while making a recipe you used to manage with your eyes closed, that might be your sign from the universe to try focusing on one thing at a time.

In my experience, I've found a huge correlation between my state of mind, my overall energy level, and my capacity to tackle difficult circumstances. And when I'm not overwhelmed by challenging situations, I'm generally more relaxed, and by extension, so is the baby.

Believe in a solution

The whole notion of believing a solution exists is often enough to jumpstart my willingness to solve a problem and feel some momentum. Take, for example, when you lose something. Apparently, it's most often very close to where you first thought it might be. So when this happens, I reassure myself by believing that it's somewhere in the house, and I just need to locate it. This can take the form of visualizing it within the house's footprint and imagining my surroundings without barriers. It's kind of like when you have laser vision in video games, and you can see through walls.

Instead of getting upset about the fact that I don't know where it is, I start by closing my eyes, thinking of where I last saw the item, and expanding my circle of search from that location until I find it. Even as I'm typing this, I realize it may sound a bit silly, but believing in a solution is oddly encouraging. Seriously, try it the next time you lose something.

Why am I telling you about this? Because it has truly changed how I approach a wide range of things since I've become a mama. It's a bit of a trick that you play on your brain. I think we sometimes give up too easily, so it's helpful in some of my hardest moments to remind myself not to fret, that a solution does exist!

And this goes beyond the physical space; I also apply this way of thinking to other problems, whether they're philosophical, emotional, financial, or family-related. It might not always be the solution you expected it to be, though . . . Food for thought.

Go on the offensive

This is all about a mindset and looking for areas of potential triumph to overcome obstacles. Opportunities can be present in every difficult situation; you just need to change your focus and make yourself aware of them.

When I first moved my daughter into her own room, I didn't fully grasp how the creaky floors would become the bane of my existence, at least for a brief but unforgettable period. You see, I would sit in a chair while my daughter fell asleep, but upon exiting the room, the noise from my footsteps would inevitably wake her up. I'll save you the long version of the story, but ultimately, this would happen repeatedly every night.

One time, I even resorted to crawling out on my hands and knees, after a friend suggested I try to distribute my weight more evenly across the noisy floor (which worked, by the way). But then I decided enough was enough and started studying the creak patterns on the floor so I could map out the least noisy spots. I then marked my escape route with masking tape X's along the floor. Is this rocket science? No. Did it give me some sense of control over the situation in which I had previously felt powerless? Yes.

This example is relatively straightforward, but it taught me an important lesson. Sometimes there's an easier fix for something than you first anticipated, and instead of accepting defeat, you can go on the offensive! That is one thing about motherhood that I've found so incredibly empowering. We're faced with so many new problems that require grit, instinctual love, and a whole lot of patience (raise your hand if you've ever tried to will your child to sleep—it simply doesn't work that way!).

Developing all these new skills, in turn, can be transferred to so many other aspects of life. I know I'm so much better at rolling with the punches now than I've ever been, and I have my daughter to thank for that.

Boundaries

It's possible that you've never really considered the place for creating boundaries in your life or the complex relationship you might have with maintaining them, but they're so important to your well-being. Take, for example, having a family that likes to drop by unannounced. Maybe this used to work for you. You liked having this open-door policy where you fed off the energy of people coming into your home and the boisterous vibe that it entailed.

But maybe with a new baby, not so much. Your needs will evolve, and it's important to be able to clearly articulate what's okay for you and what isn't. It takes a lot of courage and strength, but over time, you can get better at setting and managing boundaries in your relationships. I recommend seeking out books to read on this topic if this is something that you're interested in learning more about.

Champion your mama-self

As in, be proud of who you are as a mama. Feel good about the mama that you are today without feeling the need to justify anything. Life will be exponentially easier the moment you stop trying to be a certain type of mama or succumb to outside pressure of who you think you should be. Besides, the amount of energy it takes to be someone else isn't sustainable and can have a disastrous effect on your well-being when compounded over time.

This can sometimes be so challenging because you're trying to navigate your new identity as it unfolds daily, while being confronted with so many new situations, many of which are social. Most of the time, you probably won't have the luxury of spending as much time figuring out where you stand as you might have had in the past.

Sometimes, part of discovering who *you* are as a mama will come from being exposed to a type of mama you don't relate to. I can tell you right now you'll have some missteps, but it's all part of the process. Over time, I think most parents let go of the expectations coming from their close entourage (like immediate family) in favor of doing what's best for them. The sooner you realize this, the better.

5

CONNECTION

Be good to your person. That's probably the single best piece of advice that I can give you. Side note: if you don't currently have a partner that's actively involved in caring for the little human being in your life, feel free to skip over this chapter altogether. However, reading through it may still be beneficial if you consider *yourself* to be your person and apply some of the approaches to you.

The arrival of a new baby has a halo effect on the whole family unit. You're not the only one experiencing this tremendous shift in your life. I know it's hard enough to put yourself in someone else's shoes under normal circumstances, let alone during this time. And yes, things may be somewhat unbalanced in terms of who is addressing more direct baby-related needs at the beginning—if you're breastfeeding, for instance—but it's not like your partner is experiencing anything even remotely close to their pre-baby existence either.

For all the great and magical things that new life brings to a couple, there are also lots of less-traveled hardships that you'll experience together, some of which will be much more intense than you could've ever imagined. Remember earlier when I mentioned preparing to meet your worst self? Using the word cranky would be an understatement. And guess what, your partner will be on the receiving end of this highly inevitable eventuality, when all of your idiosyncrasies manifest in a heightened state.

Some partnerships don't survive the arrival of a child into the mix. Let me tell you, there'll be plenty of situations that could easily snowball during this fiercely intense period of your life. Sadly, although it's not impossible, it's hard to rebuild mutual respect once it has eroded beyond recognition. I strongly believe that if you keep the notion of kindness toward your partner in your heart, you'll navigate the bumps better together. Though, it won't always be easy.

On the topic of kindness, I view it as a muscle that you can work on and strengthen over time. And if you exercise your kindness regularly, you can avoid forgetting what it's like to be a nice person, which is where the danger starts. Here are some of the things that I've learned that have helped me be a better companion.

Think about what you need

The ability to communicate your needs in a partnership is critical. You know yourself best, so who better to make them known to your partner? Speaking on behalf of my experience and of so many others around me, it might take a little time before you adjust your discourse regarding your needs and learn to communicate them clearly to your partner after the arrival of a new baby. Heck, you might not even know what they are yet, and many mamas I know have a hard time giving up control of certain tasks.

There may come a time where your partner will ask you how they can better support you because they might be at a loss. Yes, in an ideal world, they would figure out what you need in every moment as it changes at the speed of light based on your current emotions, but we all know that's not how it works.

Don't forget that, ultimately, it's your responsibility to express your needs. So, when you have a moment of respite, like in the shower, take that time to think of concrete examples of how your partner can better support you. Sometimes, we are battling a feeling of being overwhelmed and don't even know where to start. But if you can visualize something that will help you, chances are you're one step closer to being able to communicate it and make it come true.

Ask your partner what they need

This is in the same vein as above and is especially important if your partner is not the best at articulating their needs. Sometimes, when we have a lot going on, it's hard—and scary even—to think about opening a can of worms by asking your partner in a very straightforward way what you can do for them. What if they start listing off a million things that they need, and then you just worry that you're adding new things to your plate that you will not be able to do for them?

The idea here is that starting a discussion will hopefully give you more overall clarity as to what the best way is to spend your energy and address the needs of your partner. Maybe you'll discover that something you thought you were doing for them wasn't something that they even wanted or needed. Perhaps the thing they preferred was much easier to accomplish.

You might get confirmation that some of the effort you're putting toward things is tremendously appreciated. Try not to run away from information. It's hard to help your partner when you don't know what they need help with, even if technically it's your partner's responsibility to communicate their own needs. If you're unsure, ask!

A note on physical touch

Having a baby may change your relationship to physical touch, with your tolerance of touch varying in degrees of intensity and duration. Although being pregnant is arguably much more intrusive in terms of direct and continuous contact, there's something that literally shifts in the universe from that first skin-to-skin experience with your baby.

Touch is fundamental to humans, no question about that, but fast-forward a few weeks or even months after the birth of your baby, and a lot of that touching, so to speak, may be limited to said baby. Here's the thing that I realized: having a baby makes you come face-to-face with all sorts of things that, in my case, I hadn't given much thought to in many years. Like how much touching I want, like, or need at any given moment. Pre-baby, if I didn't feel like snuggling on the couch with my partner, I could simply get up or move away. It was well within my control to determine how much physical contact I had in my life.

But as you know, caring for a tiny little human in those first few months is a whole other story. It involves physical contact 24/7 and limited control over it at any given time. Yet, at the same time, you're experiencing the deepest connection to another human being that you have ever felt. Your heart opens to a new type of love that you didn't even know existed, like unlocking a hidden secret level in a video game. For an infant, this new love all relates back to touch. You realize the importance of human contact as a tool for bonding and as its own language when words are not an option. The power of a hug and its inherent ability to bring tremendous comfort.

But sometimes, it can be overwhelming. It's important to remember that you and your partner are likely living two very distinct, very new relationships with physical touch, whether it pertains to the new baby or with each other. Over time, and as you adapt, don't lose sight of the importance of regaining a balance that feels right for you both, especially if it's one of your love languages.

Speak with respect

It's worthwhile to practice speaking with respect to your partner, especially in the face of the many parenting challenges that you'll face while with a newborn. Words can be a source of love, power, pain, and sadness. Be aware of the impact of your words, and try your best to speak to your partner in the way you would also like to be spoken to.

Relationship conflict is normal

Healthy relationships will have conflict. It's not about avoiding relationship conflict but rather how you navigate it. Learning how to work through conflict is one of the most important and worthwhile pursuits that you can do with your partner. Therapy is a great support for this!

Try to be flexible

It's very easy to get set in your own ways of doing something without even realizing it. Actively think about how you can be more open to your partner with regards to their actions and ideas. It's easy to fall into a habit of micromanaging things, especially if you have created an attachment to a certain way of doing things for the baby. However, inflexibility can create more stress in a relationship. Try to consciously create space for your partner where they can also feel comfortable with learning how to do things in a way they enjoy that makes sense to them when it comes to the baby.

Take a breather when needed

When conflicts arise with your partner during tense emotional moments, it's okay to ask for a bit of time to gather yourself. Maybe you've reached a point where you're not feeling heard, seen, or understood, and you're simply so hurt that only a bit of space can give you or your partner the chance to self-soothe and gain perspective.

The timing and how you communicate this need to your partner is key. It's important not to use this as a way of shutting out your partner or exerting control over the discussion, as this could incite even more conflict.

To prevent this from happening, have a chat with your partner—outside of a conflict—about the best way to take a break when conflict occurs in the future. The goal being to recognize when a conversation is no longer productive, and calm down before reconnecting with your partner to resume the discussion at a later time.

Weekly check-in

The idea here is to schedule a weekly meeting between you and your partner to assess the current division of tasks and responsibilities and to discuss upcoming events or needs to ensure that both sides are aligned. There are so many types of labor that exist in a partnership and household. Your partner may have a general appreciation for you, but it's very possible that a lot of what you do goes unnoticed. Not intentionally, of course. Just that life is busy, and sometimes we are more absorbed in what we are doing ourselves.

Finding a framework that brings to light all of the things that need to be done so that you can have a more open conversation on a regular basis can be very helpful. Consider which tasks you each prefer and may even give you energy versus the ones that require more emotional or physical strength.

Remember to be gentle on yourself and that it's not a competition. There's no prize for who does more. Both sides win with more awareness around the collective responsibilities that you're faced with and a better understanding of how to help each other tackle them.

Consider couples counseling

Speaking from my own experience, I used to have mixed feelings about the place that therapy could have in my life. Somehow, I felt more accepting of therapy in the context of resolving a specific issue for which you needed guidance. What I have learned since—and something I wish I was more open to sooner—was to think about therapy as a tool to help you grow, both individually and as a couple. You don't need to be going through huge so-called problems to justify seeking someone out to work through things.

Your ambition could also simply be that you want to be a better version of who you are. Expand your emotional awareness, do not fear showing up as who you really are, and learn how to speak up for your needs. Perhaps all it takes is someone to listen to you and ask you a few questions to make you see things from a different perspective. Sometimes, facing difficult feelings about yourself is easier with someone who can create a safe environment for you. Maybe it's not about fixing something but rather taking the time to make space for growth in your life.

Of course, your partner must also be open to doing couples therapy, as you cannot impose this upon them. The good news is that nowadays there are a lot of virtual options that are much easier to fit into a baby schedule. You could plan for the sessions to take place during a nap time in the comfort of your own home. Sometimes, it can also be nice to share thoughts on the session later that day or the following day with your partner and continue to develop the discussion.

Discover a new activity together

If you're like most people I know, your definition of what you consider to be fun or what you would want to do with your free time has probably shifted dramatically. Yes, staring at a wall in silence counts! But in all seriousness, rituals are important. Connecting is important. Sharing a laugh, no matter how silly, in the right moment, has the power to melt away so much tension.

Here's an idea to try. Make a list of activities that you would like to do with your partner that sound appealing to you, and ask your partner to do the same. Put a variety of things on the list. It can be something as simple as baking a pie, going for a walk, having a bath together, or trying something fun that you have never done. Once you each have your lists, compare them and you can each pick something from your partner's list that interests you. Try to be open to the process and the experience.

Stay curious

Remember to stay curious about you partner, just as you were when you first met them.

When you're ready, maybe you can ask them about their experience on the day your baby was born. How did it make them feel? Were there scary moments? Or on a broader level, how is parenting different than what they expected?

Sometimes, just the act of asking your partner what their experience was like at a specific life event can bring up all sorts of memories, feelings, and ideas. It allows you to connect in new ways and can help you to understand each other better.

You're on the same team

Times will get tough, and your partner might be the only other adult you interact with on a regular basis, so you may sometimes take your frustrations out on them—particularly during those early days when you're physically recovering from childbirth and your hormones are readjusting postpartum.

It's worth having a conversation with your partner early on about the kinds of physiological changes that you'll be enduring and the emotional manifestations which may result. That way your partner can familiarize themselves with the signs and recognize these natural adaptations as they happen, which may cut down on misinterpretations and fighting.

It might take a lot of effort to remember that you're on the same team, and it won't always happen organically. You may have to verbally remind yourself on occasion—yes, out loud—to apologize and take accountability for your own behavior when appropriate. This goes both ways. Try to always give your partner the benefit of the doubt, and assume their positive intentions until you know more about a situation.

6

NOURISHMENT

A new baby in the house will certainly shake things up when it comes to food. But not in the beginning of course, when their diet is limited to breastmilk or formula. Eventually, as they begin to eat solid food, they'll have a big impact on the type of food that you buy, how you cook the food, and what you eat.

A lot will depend on what your relationship to food was prior to having a baby. Is cooking something that you enjoyed or always thought of as a hassle? Would you like to spend more time in the kitchen or less? Do you feel stressed when it comes to food and are looking for ways to make your life easier? How do you envision mealtime as a family? Giving these questions some thought will help you come up with what works best for you. You don't need to have all the answers now.

My own connection to food is very much rooted in love, and feeding my family is an expression of that love. Over the last few years, it's also become a mindful practice. It's a chance for me to slow down and be present, doing something that I enjoy while being creative. Most days, being in the kitchen fills me with energy that I can bottle up and bring with me to other areas of my day. The following are some of my ideas about food and nourishment, and some useful tips and tricks that I have learned along the way.

Baby-led weaning (BLW)

This is a method of introducing solid foods to babies, starting with soft finger foods, which you let your baby feed to themself. Around six months of age, assuming your baby has hit specific milestones like sitting unassisted and holding onto objects, you can consider this option. It's good because it can help babies practice chewing and swallowing, facilitates fine motor development, and makes eating a positive experience. They become more familiar with textures and have more control over what they put in their mouths.

It's very important to offer safe foods that are not choking hazards as well as understand the different between gagging and choking. It also requires very close supervision. It's worth taking an infant CPR class to be prepared for introducing your baby to solids, whatever the stage you do it in. As you can imagine, it's very messy. To incorporate BLW at dinnertime, serve the baby one soft item that is included in your meal.

If you want to learn more about it, there are plenty of resources available online. There are also workshops that you can take with experts who are knowledgeable about the practice and can offer more personalized guidance and answer any questions that you may have. I did an in-person group class where babies were welcome to join. I attended it with a friend, and it gave me the confidence I needed to get started.

Introducing allergy foods

The guidance for introducing common allergens has evolved in recent years, so do some research to ensure that you have the latest information. To help prevent future development of allergies, the current recommendation is to introduce allergenic foods to babies that show developmental signs of readiness for solids around the age of six months.

Introduction of the major allergens include peanut, cow's milk, eggs, tree nuts, wheat, fish, shellfish, soy, and sesame. The recommendation is only to introduce one at a time, starting with peanut butter and eggs. Always start with small amounts and ensure you're avoiding hard or chunky foods that can be choking hazards.

Signs of an allergic reaction can include hives, swelling, vomiting, wheezing and difficulty breathing, to name a few. These will usually occur within minutes, or up to a couple of hours after the exposure (sometimes it can be even longer). If you have any concerns, contact your healthcare provider or go to the emergency room—it's better safe than sorry. I know some parents who have introduced peanut butter to babies while in the parking lot of a hospital because they felt safer doing so there. While that might sound a bit extreme, at the end of the day you should do what feels right for you.

Once you have successfully introduced an allergen without a reaction, the key is to keep including it as part of your baby's regular diet to help avoid the development of an allergy down the road. Meaning, at least a couple of times on a weekly basis, which, for some of the items listed above, could be a challenge, so do your best.

A doctor once told me that this is another advantage of living in France, as there tends to be more cross-contamination of ingredients within bakeries, which means everyone typically is exposed to various allergens on a regular basis, and therefore fewer allergies are developed.

Sitting to eat with your baby

It's a great idea to develop this habit from the moment your baby starts eating food. It doesn't have to be every meal at first, because sometimes it's a nice break to have the baby in a high chair while you do some practical stuff in the kitchen. But when you can, take a pause, and sit down to eat at the same time as your baby during the daytime. It creates a nice ritual and gives you the opportunity to enjoy your food instead of running around and eating on your feet.

With it comes to dinner, I encourage you to try starting a tradition of eating dinner together as a family. Yes, it means that it'll be less relaxing. But it's worth it over time, and it gets better. And to be honest, I was so tired by 7 p.m. anyway that I kind of enjoyed the early dinner aspect.

More importantly though, it's a bonding opportunity that can help your baby become a better eater and perhaps even more open to trying new foods. It's easy to create simplified versions of the food you're cooking by setting some aside before adding seasoning. The goal is to create a foundation for a healthy relationship with food for your baby. Your only job is to offer food that is healthy, and it's up to your child to determine what they want to eat and how much.

For some, this won't be possible due to work schedule limitations, and you may opt to serve two dinners on weeknights—an early one for kids and a later one for adults.

A closer look at ingredients

A big turning point in my journey with food was when I started educating myself in a more active and conscious way. Reading food labels and gaining a better understanding of the food that I was eating really empowered me to make healthier choices.

Ultimately, it led me to reduce the number of processed foods that I consume on a regular basis. Processing changes a food from its original state, and levels can vary from mild to ultra-processed. Essentially, processed foods are made by adding sugar, salt, oil, or other substances that people don't typically use at home, like preservatives, stabilizers, bulking agents, corn syrup, artificial coloring, sweeteners, and flavoring—just to name a few.

NOURISHMENT

Think about it as you begin to introduce foods to your baby. You may want to monitor or limit salt intake among other things. Lots of common foods are highly processed, such as breakfast cereals, frozen meals, meats, bread, and cheese. At a first glance, you might not see the different between some of the options that are in your grocery store, but there are plenty of alternatives for less processed foods these days with certain brands. A quick review of the labels can help you make the best choice for your family.

Where possible, I favor whole foods or foods as close to their natural state as possible. I like to think that if it doesn't require a label, that's a good sign. Overall though, I typically follow an 80/20 rule on this so that I don't become too rigid around food. Meaning I aim for 80 percent of what I eat to be clean or minimally processed food, and for the other 20 percent I give myself some freedom to eat whatever food makes sense, without feeling badly or having to justify it to myself. If I am in a social setting or travelling, and therefore have less control over my food, I adjust the ratio to give myself more flexibility and account for my circumstances.

Postpartum nutrition

It's important to nourish your body with healthy foods, as this is a key part of your ongoing recovery. Well-rounded meals with a wide variety of foods are recommended, such as protein, fruits, vegetables, nuts, seeds, whole grains, and healthy fats. They can also help boost milk supply. If you're breastfeeding, you'll require additional calories every day. Remember that food intake should always factor in your level of physical activity, which may be different postpartum.

The demands of early motherhood can often lead to inconsistent eating and mealtimes. If your daily routine is feeling a little chaotic, and you're not getting all the nutrients that you should be, supplementing with vitamins can be an avenue to discuss with your healthcare provider or naturopath.

Whether we like to admit it or not, there remains societal pressure when it comes to returning to prepregnancy weight and size. Unfortunately, this can lead some to make food choices that can slow down recovery and make their days much harder, both emotionally and physically, especially if calories are being restricted and energy levels are affected. Educating yourself about healthy approaches to losing postpartum weight is key. My advice to you is to be patient and give yourself time. For those looking for a comprehensive personalized plan to meet individual needs, a nutritionist can help with that.

NOURISHMENT

Daily green love

When I first started making green juice, it wasn't as readily available as it is today in grocery stores, cafés, and restaurants. It has gained a lot of popularity in the last few years, and there are so many varieties, recipes, and methods available now. If you haven't tried it, it's a drink that is made from the juices of vegetables, primarily green ones. Often, fruit is added for taste, or other ingredients like cayenne and ginger. It's a way of bringing nutrients to a balanced diet and is not meant to be consumed exclusively.

I was an avid juicer before I had a baby. Although it doesn't take that long to make at home, it does involve some prepping and cleaning. After I had a baby, it just wasn't realistic to continue making it every day. I started making larger juice batches, enough for two weeks' worth, and freezing them in individual portions. Defrosted green juice doesn't quite taste as good as when it's freshly made, but it serves as the perfect base for a green smoothie. I would add a few other key ingredients like banana, avocado, spirulina and wheatgrass and give it a good blend!

I'm sharing this example in part because if you haven't tried green juice, I highly recommend it, but also, because I wanted to share an example of not giving up on something that doesn't quite fit in the same way after you've had a baby.

If there's something that you love eating, drinking, or doing, think about how you can hack it or modify it slightly to fit your present needs. You certainly don't have to give up on it. Even my solution is not for everyone. Maybe you would prefer to buy green juice for a few months to tide you over. Either way, you have options.

Hidden snacks

This is self-explanatory, but basically find spots all over your home to stash nonperishable snacks that you may need to access in a pinch when you're hungry—or hangry—and desperately need to eat something. Odds are, the moment the baby falls asleep in your arms, everything becomes quiet. You finally have a moment to take a deep breath and relax, and you'll realize that you're starving.

One thing I know is, when you're tired, everything is harder. When you're *tired and hungry*, well, it certainly isn't easier. On any given day, you'll be juggling so many balls that there's just no way to anticipate everything that you'll need all the time. Raw almonds were my go-to. Buy a huge bag, divide into smaller, snack-sized portions, and find spots where you tend to dwell when you have the baby—maybe the bedroom night table, or the drawer in the changing table. I also kept some in the diaper bag and stroller compartments, and I even had a jar full of them on the coffee table.

Costco, how I love thee

Buying in bulk can be really useful when it comes to certain food items that you consume regularly. Why I particularly love Costco is because they have products that cannot be found elsewhere and have great overall value. They also deliver groceries to your home and have a generous return policy (I've heard of a woman returning a half-eaten chicken). But most importantly, they have plenty of organic food at very reasonable prices. In fact, Costco invests in the development in organic farming and helps farmers grow more supply in exchange for first rights to buy organic produce from the farmers. I can attest to the quality of their produce from personal experience! If you don't have a membership, consider going with a friend to check it out before committing.

Befriend your freezer

If you haven't yet experienced the many joys of how useful your freezer can truly be, let me break it down for you. Think of it as a tool to give you more flexibility. It can do so much more than just storing food that you bought in the freezer section.

First off, it's a great way to keep small portions of leftover ingredients that would likely go bad before you need them if you kept them in the fridge. For liquids, you can freeze them in an ice cube tray and transfer them to a bag when frozen—things like heavy cream, pesto, wine, coconut milk, stock, citrus juice. Having them in smaller, more accessible sizes means that it's super easy to add them to sauces, water, or salad dressing. Other items that can freeze well are cooked rice, chickpeas, leftover tomato paste, and ginger. Lemons and limes are even easier to zest from frozen and will release more juice when thawed.

If you have some leafy greens that are about to go bad, you can freeze them for easy use in a smoothie later. I keep frozen banana chunks and avocado halves for the same purpose. I also use the bananas for baking, as it seems like I never have very ripe bananas on hand when I am in the mood to bake banana bread—the freezer is a great solution for that!

I recommend freezing small individual portions of leftovers that can be easily reheated in the microwave. This is great for leftovers that have lost their appeal. You'll be happier to find them in your freezer in a couple of weeks!

When it comes to sweets, here are a couple of ideas. When you have leftover cake, you can individually wrap slices to enjoy for months afterward. Some days, it was very comforting to know that I had a slice of chocolate cake with my name on it waiting for me in the freezer, I won't lie. It's also a great place to store cookies to keep them fresh. They only take a few minutes to defrost on the counter. You can freeze big batches and then you always have something homemade on hand if you have unexpected visitors.

The freezer is also a great tool for storing food and meals for baby, like mashed vegetables. A hack I learned from my aunt was freezing elbow macaroni in small plastic bags. When you need quick pasta on hand for baby, all you need to do is remove the macaroni from the bag, place it in a strainer, and pour boiling water over it from a kettle. Add a sauce of your choice or butter, and you're good to go!

If you're unsure if something can be frozen, give it a try! My mother freezes all sorts of things that I will probably never attempt myself—the texture of some things like milk can change and that's a no go for me—but I do like the approach of at least seeing if it works. When it involves meat, do some research online if you're unsure. I know that it's not a good idea to refreeze uncooked raw meat that has previously been frozen, for example. Beyond that, try to keep track of what's in your freezer, or at least have a peek occasionally to make sure you haven't forgotten something. You can always keep an inventory list, but I've never been that organized.

Weekly baking

This is a habit that grew on me over time. It's a nice, calm activity to do with the baby nearby, or while listening to a podcast during their nap. You can easily make baby-friendly variations of things like breakfast muffins by substituting the sugar with apple sauce. Oddly enough, sometimes baking can give you a feeling of control over something small at a time when you may need it.

Sheet-pan meals

If you haven't yet tried these, they're the best. It's like those one-pot recipes, but in this case, it's even easier because you just put everything on one roasting sheet. They usually only take about twenty minutes to bake, and there's minimal food prep involved. They're good for those days when you just don't have a lot of inspiration and want something easy and tasty. There are plenty of ideas online and tons of cookbooks about these with so many variations. My go-to was sausages cut into one-inch pieces, chopped up bell peppers, and onions. Toss everything with some olive oil and oregano. You can always serve it with rice on the side or a salad. Voilà, dinner!

Easy as 1-2-3

There's no shame in simple cooking. In fact, I love it. Making food that has very few ingredients is one of my favorite things to do. I often try to simplify my own recipes just to try it out. The reason being, it's just easier. Less ingredients to remember to buy, to have on hand, and to remember to add, and fewer steps to get to the final result. Don't get me wrong, I love cooking an elaborate meal that requires several hours and lots of effort for special occasions. But it's important to remember that simplicity can be so useful in the day-to-day.

The key here is not to feel guilty about the fact that you're cutting corners but rather that you're proud to be able to make something edible with only a few ingredients. This approach can be a useful tool to be gentle on yourself and use when you don't need extra pressure in your life, especially when you're already feeling overwhelmed.

Some of my favorite four-or-five-ingredient recipes include chicken potpie (rotisserie chicken, cream cheese, chicken stock, frozen vegetables, and crust) and peanut butter cookies (peanut butter, unsweetened shredded coconut, egg, sugar). Once you start down this path, it becomes easier to enjoy the simplicity. Remember to document your successes if you're like me and tend to forget. You can keep a note or create a photo album on your phone.

Slow cooking for the win

Slow cooking is amazing. There, I said it. Basically, it involves simmering food at a low temperature over several hours. You can do this at home with your stove, but there exists a countertop appliance called a slow cooker (or Crock-Pot) that makes things a little easier and more hands off. You can set it to cook for a specific amount of time, after which it'll switch to warm to keep food ready. Typically, food is cooked on the low setting for about eight hours. It's a great method for soups, stews, and softening tough cuts of meat, but I've also used mine to make lasagna, meatloaf, brownies, pineapple chicken, stuffed peppers, ribs, and the list goes on.

The reason I mention it here is because it's a very useful and relatively inexpensive appliance to have, and such a practical way to make dinner when you have a baby. It doesn't use a lot of electricity. You can prep during nap time and then basically be hands off until dinnertime. It can be great for the baby too because it creates very soft and tender food. It's only one pot to clean at the end of the night. Some recipes require searing some meat for extra flavor as a step before you put it in the slow cooker, so you need to have a stomach to do that in the morning (full disclosure).

It's also practical if you're going back to work, as some recipes are okay to prep and keep in the fridge overnight. Before you decide to freestyle variations of your own recipes adapted for the slow cooker, it's important to understand the role that moisture plays, as it doesn't escape while cooking.

Meal planning can help

This involves planning a weekly or monthly menu in advance. It takes more energy to do at first, but over time it, can help reduce stress around meals, ensure that you consume more variety of nutrients, and can even become something that you enjoy doing, promise! If you're looking for inspiration, there are plenty of resources online, especially when it comes to meal planning or quick and easy recipes.

The first step is to pick a method to keep track and help you stay organized. If you prefer writing things down, you can opt for a notebook. You can also get a board that you hang somewhere in the kitchen. If you're more inclined to use online tools, there are plenty of options to consider. I use a calendar template in Google Sheets so that I can access it while I'm on the go. But I also write out the weekly meals on a whiteboard so that I can easily reference it throughout the week.

I recommend putting together your grocery list while meal planning or right afterward. It makes grocery shopping much simpler, whether you're doing it online or in person. It's also easier to avoid overbuying items you don't need.

It's a nice idea to get input from your partner to incorporate their likes. It goes without saying that you don't have to be the designated meal planner in the household. It can just as easily be your partner's task or a collaborative thing. The same goes for cooking the meals and buying groceries. It's very easy to split these tasks up in a way that makes sense for everyone.

If you feel stuck and are out of ideas, consider doing recurring theme meal days. For example, Pizza Friday is a nice ritual. You can buy dough and rotate toppings, and it's quick to bake. I've heard of people picking categories every day of the week, like meatless Mondays or taco Tuesdays, meal salad Wednesdays, pasta Thursdays . . . You get the gist. Then, you only have to come up with a different variation within a category.

I highly recommend keeping some sort of meal database of the successes, so you can refer to it when needed. Because no matter how good your memory is, it'll be hard to keep track. I keep a note on my phone and like to group mine by category (main, pizza, side dish). Over time, it'll become a very handy resource. You can even save online links to favorite recipes for easy access.

Batch cooking

Basically, this means cooking in larger quantities so that you can keep some for a later date. There are many different ways of doing this, and therefore it can take a bit of time to understand what works best for you, but it's so worth it. The easiest way to get started is by doubling up meals when you cook them, and either refrigerate or freeze the rest.

The main idea is that cooking this way will save you time, help you to make healthy meals, and save money with bulk buying. While it's undoubtedly an efficient approach, you must invest time up front to be able to benefit from less cooking and cleaning on a daily basis. Soup, pasta sauces, chili, lasagna, meatballs, and casseroles are all great options for batch cooking.

Batch prepping is also something to consider. When buying larger quantities of meat or fish, I started this trick of marinating the protein, portioning into bags, and freezing it uncooked for easy use later. Cutting chicken or salmon into cubes makes it faster to defrost and cook when you're ready to incorporate them into a meal. You can also batch prep certain ingredients that typically take longer to prepare, so you'll have them on hand for a later time when you need them as ingredients within other recipes.

Repurpose leftovers

There are so many ways to get creative with leftovers and create great new meals. Rotisserie chicken can become fajitas. You can make a weekly stir-fry using uneaten rice and veggies. Mashed potatoes can be used for shepherd's pie. Adding cheese to leftovers and baking them is always a win. You can make bowls for lunch with almost anything. Roasted veggies can be used as toppings for pizza, or better yet, they can be incorporated into a sandwich. Sometimes just taking a more intentional approach to leftovers can make them feel as exciting as making new food. You can even pre-plan having specific leftovers for a variation of a meal later in the week.

Try to limit food waste

This takes practice and requires paying some attention to your habits to understand the biggest drivers of food waste in your home. Take your time, and just have a goal of improving instead of a zero-waste policy, because that will not set you up for success and likely will only make you feel badly.

NOURISHMENT

An easy way to get started is simply to gain better awareness of the situation. Take notes on which items you tend to throw away on any given day. You can keep a little notepad by the fridge. You'll hopefully notice some trends over a few weeks. Some things will jump out at you and be super easy fixes.

Bagged lettuce is one of the most common things that people throw out. Because the moisture is trapped, it has a limited optimal lifespan, even if you try to extend it by adding paper towel. Let's face it, having a new baby requires flexibility, and no matter what your intentions are when you buy your food, it's quite normal if you don't end up using it on the day you expected, or even if you end up forgetting about it in the fridge. An alternative would be to pick a heartier green that will likely stay fresh longer, like arugula, baby kale, or spinach.

If you find yourself throwing away leftovers that have gone bad, perhaps it's just a question of timing and being better about freezing them earlier. Typically, leftovers last about five days, so if you're in doubt on whether they'll get eaten (after all, it's hard to predict the eating habits of your partner), just freeze them! You can always defrost and reheat them. As mentioned earlier, same goes for produce that's about to go bad or for random small, prepped ingredients that you don't expect to have a use for in the short term. Toss them in the freezer for a later use.

My all-time, hands down favorite way to limit food waste is something called Touski. It's an amalgamation of sorts from the French phrase, "Tout ce qu'il reste dans le frigo," which means: "Everything left in the fridge." Towards the end of each week, I like to have a Touski night to help get rid of all the random small portions of food in the fridge. It can become a theme night where it's fun to eat a collection of things that don't usually go together. You can even put it all on one large wooden cutting board to make it fancy. Give it a try!

It's okay if you lose interest in cooking

This is completely normal. If you used to love being in the kitchen and spend hours cooking, but you don't have the same zest for it at the moment, give yourself some time. You're caring for a baby and learning so many new skills. Your brain might be overstimulated and just needs to rest when possible, especially considering the fact that you're probably not sleeping a ton. Don't force yourself back into that mode until you feel the desire again. Of course, you'll still likely need to cook, but don't go overboard.

NOURISHMENT

It's easy to be overwhelmed by even something as simple as a fridge full of uncooked food that's going bad every day that passes. In the meantime, look for ways to simplify and not put any additional and avoidable pressure on yourself.

That can mean buying less fresh produce and opting for frozen vegetables, because that can give you more flexibility in deciding when it's the right time to cook it, rather than being worried about expiry dates. Or you can try getting meal kits delivered with easy-to-prep meals and fewer trips to the grocery store. There are also local companies that deliver ready-made food that only needs to be reheated. Do what you need to do to feed yourself and your family.

7

MOVEMENT

After the birth of the baby, you may be eager to return to prepregnancy habits and routines, and for many, this includes exercise. The timeframe is different for everyone, depending on your preferences, the type of birth, and if you had any complications. Postpartum exercise has both mental and physical benefits. It can help to boost mood and energy, relieve stress, promote better sleep, and maintain strength during motherhood. Your healthcare provider is the best resource to determine when it's okay to resume various activities, give you recommendations around specific types of workouts, and provide guidance for your specific situation.

Start gradually. It's very important to pay attention to how you feel, as it's a good indicator of whether you're pushing yourself too hard, which can have an impact on your recovery. Making time for regular movement and exercise is an intentional act that requires effort and sometimes planning, so keep this in mind. If you're having trouble finding the time, talk to your partner to see how they can support you.

Some new mothers may experience an emotional struggle to accept the value and importance of exercise, which is very understandable. I would suggest starting with something very low impact and easy, like a daily walk. It doesn't require much preparation or equipment, and you can bring the baby.

Over time, as you work your way up to longer walks, you could consider walking with another new mom. There's something about doing an easy motion together in unison that is calming and a great backdrop for connection. Here are some other ideas in the areas of movement that you might consider trying for the first time, or rediscovering.

Dancing with baby

You won't be a stranger to using movement with your body to soothe and rock your baby in those early days after birth. Taking it one step further, dancing with your baby to music is a fun bonding activity to try at home or on a playdate with other moms. There are even mom and baby dancing group meetups. It's also a great way to socialize the baby, stimulate their senses, and help promote gentle movement. And for those times when you're going through some challenges, it can also serve to feel and release emotions.

Baby yoga

This is a great activity that you can do with your baby, as they can be actively involved in the class with some simple stretches. Some classes focus more on the baby, while others are geared toward mothers. It's a good idea to try a class before your baby is mobile, as it can be a little harder to keep them next to you when they are eager to explore and touch everything.

I was very lucky to find a small, intimate group that met weekly for yoga. After the class, we would all head over to a local coffee shop, including the teacher, to chat and connect. I have the fondest memories of this time and keep in touch with the mamas that I met during the experience. Finding these classes should be straightforward online, but don't forget to check out local boards and ask around when interacting with other new moms.

Baby swimming

This is also a great option to consider while factoring in minimum age guidelines for infants. There are many companies that offer classes, and they are typically very short. You can opt to be in the water with the baby or not, depending on your level of comfort. Babies can learn water skills and safety through play and song. If you prefer to introduce your baby to water yourself, look out for free swim times at your local pool or community center.

Mommy and baby workouts

There's no shortage of videos and ideas online for exercises that you can do with your baby while holding them, like walking lunges, baby bench presses, and squats, to name a few. Just make sure to take precautions to ensure that you can do them safely with the baby and that they've reached certain milestones, like neck control. The great thing about working out with your baby is that you have lots of flexibility to do it when it works for your schedule and baby's nap schedule. It also requires very little equipment.

Stroller workouts

If you're looking for a more physically demanding activity, this is it. There are groups that offer classes outside and can include all sorts of exercises, from strength to cardio to core training. If you or your partner are into running, you can consider purchasing a stroller that is designed for it. It's a great option for baby naps too, and to give you some valuable alone time while your partner is out of the house on a run with the baby.

Babywearing exercises

If you love babywearing, you can easily incorporate exercises into your daily routines. You have a little more mobility and freedom to use your arms so you can explore other types of movements and even incorporate dumbbells. It's especially important to be attuned to how you and your body are feeling, as working out while wearing a baby can be very demanding on your core.

Activity trackers

If you're someone that likes to keep track of exercise and can use that as a tool for motivation, it's worth considering wearable activity trackers. They can also help promote personal accountability toward goals. There are many options on the market that include useful functionalities like reminders to move and visual progress charting. They can also connect to other devices and track sleep and nutrition intake. It's a good option for those that are feeling overwhelmed with the idea of exercising. You can start by simply recording the steps that you take on any given day, and set a goal to gently increase them over time.

Health and fitness apps

These can serve as a broader tool to accomplish your goals and incorporate exercise and healthy habits into your daily life. It's a more affordable alternative to hiring a personal trainer. As technology evolves, the options get better, and there are a ton of ways to personalize workouts to suit your needs. And most importantly, it gives you the freedom and flexibility to exercise when it's convenient for your schedule.

Forest bathing

So technically, there's no water involved. Forest bathing is about surrounding yourself in a forest, where the trees act as the water, and you take in all the amazing and beautiful things that it has to offer. It's a great alternative to get exercise without doing a workout routine. Using nature as a backdrop can be more appealing to some than working out at home. It's a great activity to do as a family.

8

REST

When it comes to rest, my advice is to focus on what's within your control, and try to create the best possible environment to be able to handle this part of motherhood, both mentally and physically.

During the times where I was very sleep-deprived due to the irregular sleeping patterns of my baby, it really helped me to be connected to someone that was going through similar challenges at the same time or had gone through it recently and could offer some guidance. In the moments I felt especially powerless when it came to my sleep and the baby's sleep, it helped me to take small actions that made me feel like I was at least learning or on a path toward making the situation better.

If you're going through this right now, I want you to take a moment to pause and recognize that you may be living something very hard. I can assure you that sleep deprivation will not last forever. It's a blip on the spectrum of time, even if it doesn't feel that way right now. Here are a few ideas to think about or try on the topic of optimizing rest, starting with you, and of course, the baby.

Sleeping when the baby sleeps

You will likely hear this advice from many different sources around you. For some, this works magically, and for others, it never does. Either way, give it a try, and don't be too hard on yourself if you don't succeed. I never quite managed to do this. I wasn't always in the right frame of mind to sleep when the baby was sleeping and often preferred to do something else. And when I did want to sleep, just as I was about to doze off, the baby would need me. In any case, being aware of your audience when giving your opinion on this matter is wise. You never know what the other person might be experiencing, and it can be very triggering for some to hear advice of this nature.

Limit your water before bedtime

Drinking water before bed can be disruptive for your sleep. Try to limit how much water and other fluids that you drink at least two hours before your bedtime if you want to avoid waking up at night to use the washroom. It will probably take some practice, especially if you're trying to stay hydrated and may have forgotten to drink earlier in the day.

Sleep mask

The trick is to find one that fits right, not too tight, not too loose, and preferably made of a material that's soft and breathable, like silk. For a little while there, my sleep mask was my most prized possession, not even joking. I can be quite sensitive to light impacting my sleep at times, and my eye mask was a life saver. Basically, I would keep one handy among my pillows in my bed, and then if I needed to grab it in the middle of the night, I could do it relatively quickly and without waking up too much. It's not just about blocking out the light; I think over time I created a sleep association with it, because it acts as a little blocker of the outside world and forces you to close your eyes while being cozy at the same time.

Bedtime ritual

The goal here is to develop a routine that is relaxing in preparation for bed. Doing the same things every night will help you disconnect and transition to the next part of your day. They can include things like listening to music, reading, taking a bath, or doing a skin-care routine. The trick is to be intentional about it, so give it some thought, and try out a few things.

Sleepcasts

Think of them as podcasts, but instead of their usual form, they're designed to promote sleep for adults. There are a ton of options out there, from soothing music to fall asleep, to specific sounds that are calming like ocean waves, rainfall, or guided sleep meditations. They can really help to wind down at bedtime or in the middle of the night, to help you fall back asleep after the baby does the same.

Mama sleep schedule

Thinking about and planning your baby's sleep schedule will be an ongoing part of your life. However, it's important not to forget about yourself and look for opportunities to maximize rest, especially when you're experiencing fluctuating sleep hours. Early motherhood is such a busy time, and at the end of the day, it'll be very hard to balance your need for alone time to recharge and sleep. Creating a self-boundary by setting a bedtime cutoff for yourself can help establish a healthier sleep routine.

Alternative arrangements

Some families will choose alternative short-term sleeping arrangements where partners sleep in a separate bed for the greater benefit of all during transitions and other challenging times, like when the baby is teething. It can be hard to imagine for some, but it's worth considering. Sometimes it's best to have one partner that's well rested to help support during the day, instead of two people that are equally sleep-deprived.

Avoid heavy food at bedtime

It's a good idea to give your body time to digest before bed, as heavy foods can cause indigestion, heartburn, and other issues. If I'm hungry before bed, my go-to is a bowl of cereal. Cheese and nuts are also great options.

Caffeine

Be aware of your caffeine intake and whether it's impacting your sleep. If you find yourself yawning all day yet have the energy of a thousand suns the moment your head hits the pillow, maybe it's worth looking into when you had your last coffee and setting some limits on when or how much to have.

Weighted blanket

It's a heavy blanket that helps to reduce stress and promote better sleep for some. The main idea of weighted blankets is that they have a calming effect by exerting some pressure on the body. The right one for you will depend on your own body weight. They're not meant for babies. I found mine helpful as a tool to help me fall back asleep in the middle of the night. The only downside really was that it's not the most practical thing to travel with.

Comfort is important

Assess the current situation with your mattress. Is your bed causing you or your partner any physical pain? What about your bedding and comforter? When was the last time you washed your pillows? All these things can help you get better sleep, and it's important to think about them. Do you find yourself fighting over the covers with your partner in the middle of the night, or do you have different needs when it comes to how warm each of you are? Perhaps it's worth considering the Scandinavian method of having two duvets on one shared bed. It's quite genius and can really improve the quality of your sleep.

Sleep environment

When you go into your bedroom at night, does it feel inviting? Messiness in early motherhood is normal. You'll have so much extra laundry piling up everywhere. I know I used the bassinet as a place to collect anything random I didn't have a place for after the baby grew out of it.

The thing to determine is whether the state of your bedroom is impacting your state of calm when you're going to bed or not. We all have different levels of tolerance, and yours might not be the same as your partner's. If you're finding that the mess is affecting you, see what small actions you can take, and discuss it with your partner to make sure they understand what you're hoping to do, so they don't work against you unintentionally. It can be as simple as determining that a certain area will remain clutter-free or finding a new place to store all those extra pillows temporarily if you're not making your bed every day.

Nightlights

My favorite use of them is to light the way to the bathroom or other areas of your house, like the kitchen. So, when you're half asleep, they help you to navigate your home without turning on a harsh light that may cause you to fully wake up. Which, if you need to go back to sleep, can be a problem. You can get motion-sensing ones that light up automatically when the room is dark or babyproof ones that don't get hot.

Night doula

The role of a night doula is to help care for Mom and baby in the middle of the night. It's someone that you hire to help support during a specific timeframe. They can offer relief as an extra set of hands so that you can get more rest.

In those first few months, it can be very comforting to have someone close by with experience, especially if you do not have family nearby.

Bedroom temperature

A simple indoor thermometer in the baby's bedroom can be very reassuring, especially in those periods of extreme weather, like heat waves or cold snaps. You can easily glance over and ensure it's within the right range at bedtime or in the middle of the night. When you're confident that the baby is dressed appropriately for the temperature of the room, it's one less thing to worry about if the baby wakes up in the middle of the night and you're trying to tend to their needs. And while you're at it, why not make sure your own bedroom temperature is working for you and adjust if needed to help promote better sleep?

Window treatments

Light can greatly impact sleep, and the ability to create a consistently dark room is key, both for you and your baby. Blackout curtains were very much a worthwhile purchase; you can even get portable ones to use for travel. There are also portable pods that can help to create a dark space for the baby to sleep in when visiting family or room sharing with the baby. In a pinch, you can always tape black garbage bags over the windows.

REST

Extra crib bedding layers

Layering a waterproof mattress protector followed by a sheet and then another waterproof mattress protector and another sheet is an amazing, time-saving measure. This will help minimize sleep disruption when unexpected and unfortunate events occur that require changing the bedding in the crib in the middle of the night. It's easy to simply remove the soiled set without having to fumble in the darkness to replace new bedding on the mattress. I usually even add a second waterproof mattress protector on the bottom, just for good measure. Another trick is having the extra set of clean bedding for the baby in a separate place, away from other bedding, so that it's easier to access in the night without searching through piles of sheets.

Baby's naptime

Outside of the napping honeymoon stage when your baby is a newborn—only in hindsight did I truly realize how special that was—nap time is a double-edged sword. Meaning, it can be both the greatest thing and the most frustrating thing, or both at the same time. The best word to describe nap time would be impermanence. It's constantly evolving, whether your baby is going from three naps a day to two, to one, or (gasp!) to none.

What works one day to put them down may fail hopelessly the next. How long they'll sleep during any given nap will change faster than you can say cowabunga. Some days, they won't nap, for no apparent reason, even when all elements have stayed the same. I will also add that time has a way of speeding up while the baby is sleeping. When your baby does end up going down for a nap, here's the advice I have for you.

In the first several minutes, just enjoy being able to sit without needing to worry about anything immediate, and savor the fact that your baby is peacefully resting. It's great to just take a moment to ground yourself and breathe deeply.

Without rushing, think about how you'd like to spend the time you have during the baby's nap. When was the last time you ate or drank water? What would bring you the most joy? Try to put yourself first when you think about all the things you could do and not just think about your long, mental to-do list. It's not the time to be super mom. I recommend picking something that is harder to do when the baby is awake, like showering, reading, sleeping, or spending time on a personal interest or project. Getting under a blanket to watch some reality television is a perfectly acceptable use of time. Remember your self-care.

It could be a nice time to call a friend or family member to catch up. A ten-minute phone call full of love can change the type of day you're having. It can completely re-energize you and give you something that you didn't even know you needed.

And if you find yourself checking the monitor and missing your baby, that's a normal reaction too. You and your baby are each other's worlds right now, and it can feel strange to be separated.

Sleep training

This is essentially the practice of teaching your baby to fall asleep. There are many different approaches on a wide spectrum that families may consider, from cry-it-out to more gentle methods. The timing of when to begin sleep training is another variable that differs greatly among parents. Some may opt to avoid sleep training all together. It's a personal choice, but remember to be open, as your thoughts and opinions on the topic may evolve. I know several people that had a certain position and changed it drastically once they had some experience with sleep training their own baby, and that is perfectly understandable.

I read a book that changed my whole perspective on sleep. It was called *The Happy Sleeper*, by Heather Turgeon and Julie

Wright. It's a science-backed guide that made me realize that babies want to sleep, even if it can feel like the opposite sometimes. I have recommended it to almost everybody I know with a new baby. It's been life-changing for so many new parents in my entourage, and I'm committed to keeping on spreading the word. Outside of books, there are other options to consider if you're looking for help. You can hire a sleep consultant, either privately or as a group. You can also purchase online courses.

It's important to remember that if something isn't working or you don't feel comfortable with an approach, don't feel pressured into doing it. There are moments that can be overwhelming, but it's fine to take a pause and revisit another time when you're up for it. Make sure to discuss all your concerns with your partner to ensure that you're understood and on the same page.

Sleep myths

Beware of sleep myths or unrealistic expectations that you may be placing on yourself. This includes at what age your baby should be sleeping through the night, how daytime naps can affect night sleep, or ideal bedtimes. New moms often feel pressure to stop nursing babies to sleep by a certain age. Trust your instincts because you know your baby best, and you'll learn over time what their specific likes and needs are and how best to respond to them.

Swaddling

It's an old practice of wrapping babies tightly in a blanket to restrict movement and can be very soothing for some babies. Swaddling can also help with the baby's startle reflex. There are plenty of videos online to learn how to swaddle safely. It never really worked for me, but I will admit I didn't fully invest in learning properly. I do know many people that swear by it, so do your research and try it if it sounds right for you.

Sleep sacks

This is a wearable blanket for babies that can't be kicked off during the night and is therefore a safe option as an alternative to blankets, which can pose a safety hazard. Sleep sacks usually have a little pouch at the bottom, which allows for freedom of movement of the legs. There are some that have little armholes for when the baby gets a little older. Overall, they're a great option for providing warm comfort, and they come in a variety of sizes and TOG ratings. TOG means thermal overall grade, and it refers to the warmth of the fabric. The higher the TOG, the warmer the sleep sack. For safety reasons, it's important to ensure that you're using the right size. If the sleep sack is too large, your baby can slide down and overheat or even suffocate.

Multiple pacifiers in the crib

This is a hack to prevent you having to go in several times in the night when your baby has lost their pacifier somewhere in the crib. If you spread out five extra pacifiers, they can usually find a new one within reach, use it to self-soothe, and fall back asleep more easily.

Sound machines

These are little machines that you can buy and place in the baby's room that can play a variety of sounds like white noise, birds, or even shushing to help mask environmental noises outside of the baby's room. They can become a positive sleep association for your baby as part of their bedtime routine and help them fall asleep and stay asleep. Many are multifunctional and can include lights, timers, and all sorts of other capabilities.

Teething

When your baby is in the process of growing a new tooth, it can really disrupt their sleep, given the pain associated with it—which is understandable; I can only imagine what it would feel like. Typical symptoms of teething include drooling, irritability, ear-rubbing, decreased appetite, and fever. Your baby might need extra soothing during this time and experience some extra night wake-ups. Don't be too worried about adapting your methods to provide extra comfort during this time. There are some home remedies that you can consider during waking hours too, like massaging baby's gums or applying a cold washcloth. Luckily, the teething period for each new tooth doesn't last too long, and you can resume your normal sleep routines afterwards.

Safe infant sleep

There are steps that you can take to reduce the risk of sudden infant death syndrome (SIDS), which is when a healthy baby dies without a known cause in their sleep. Placing a baby on its back when sleeping and sharing a room with the baby for the first six months are ways to lower the risk, in addition to being smoke-free. It's also important to ensure that your baby has a safe space to sleep to avoid suffocation, like sleeping on a firm, flat surface and making sure there are no loose blankets, pillows, or toys in the crib.

Outside of the crib, there are other places where the baby will fall asleep, and it's important to be extra careful, as they're not recommended places for the baby to sleep, such as nursing pillows, inclined sleepers, or baby swings. Educating yourself on safe sleep, along with educating friends, family, or any caregiver that will be in contact with your baby, is critical.

Manage worry

For many, those moments before bedtime when you finally do relax can be a prime time for all sorts of worrying to pop up, especially if you tend to be an anxious person during this time where there are many daily stressors.

See if there are any stimulants that you can eliminate before bed that might be aggravating the situation, like the use of electronics. Sometimes watching intense or scary shows can leave you with hard emotions, and because of this, they're worth avoiding. For some, it can help to write something down that you can refer to the next day. For example, if your mind is very busy thinking about all the things you must remember to do, writing down your thoughts or the next day's tasks could be a way to set aside those thoughts with more ease.

If you think you may have a more serious underlying issue with regards to sleep, such as insomnia, don't hesitate to speak to your healthcare provider to determine if a treatment plan would be helpful.

9

APPAREL

Resist the urge to put away your maternity clothes immediately, as they can be very useful in the first few months when your body will be changing. In addition, there'll be a whole new range of clothes that will be useful during the postpartum period that you may have never considered before.

When it comes to your prepregnancy clothes, it's very possible that some items will never fit the same way again, as some parts of your body, like your ribs and hips, may be permanently wider. It may be hard to let go of certain items that are meaningful. Consider seeing if a tailor can help to make some adjustments so you can keep wearing those favorite items.

Your shoe size can also change permanently after birth, and as a result, you may require a larger size. There are options to stretch out certain types of shoes with a cobbler, but you may have to consider buying new sizes altogether. I know, I know. Woe is us.

Your breasts will also go through various phases of swelling and increases in size if you're breastfeeding. It's possible to end up with a smaller breast size than you had prepregnancy. This can pose many challenges, as you'll want to feel comfortable at all stages, and it's hard to avoid having to purchase many different bra sizes. Here are my tips and tricks when it comes to apparel and footwear. Comfort, accessibility, functionality, and simplicity are the main drivers behind my recommendations.

Hero outfits

You know how some people always dress the same? Well, this is a darn good postpartum strategy. Some outfits are just more effortless and make you feel good. There's no rule that says you need to have a minimum amount of variety in your outfits. Most people probably won't notice, and your baby certainly won't. The key is embracing this versus feeling badly about it. You really only need a few outfits, and you can buy multiples of your favorite joggers and tops.

Specialty bras

Bras that are designed for easy access for pumping and nursing can make your life so much easier. They typically have extra built-in support to handle heavy breasts when your milk comes in. They also have flaps that can be unlatched to expose the nipple easily. It's common to wear bras frequently in the first weeks, even overnight, until your supply evens out. It's normal to experience leaking, and you may need to wear nursing pads inside of your bra.

Leakproof underwear

It's safest to wait to wear a tampon until at least six weeks after birth. Leakproof underwear are a great alternative to pads while you're bleeding postpartum. There are great options that can absorb up to ten tampons, worth of liquid and can be worn during the day and overnight. There are so many styles available. My personal favorite are leakproof shorts with super absorbency.

Robes

Robes are great because they come in so many different styles, materials, and lengths, so you have many options to choose from. I recommend a robe that has good coverage, with pockets if possible. They're great for nursing and pumping and very cozy. They also offer plenty of room for a changing body.

House dresses

House dresses are basically dresses that were originally meant to be worn for simple household chores and quick errands. They are breathable and comfortable and have regained popularity over the last few years, and for good reason. They're a perfect alternative to athleisure if you want something a bit more stylish that's also comfortable to nap in. It's a super easy option to have in your closet if you love dresses.

Basic V-necks

They're a great basic essential to have that are also nursing friendly. They're relatively inexpensive and easy to find. It's great to stock on up these to wear every day, as you'll experience a lot of baby fluids on your clothes and don't have to feel too badly about having to toss a few.

Leggings

These are a must. They're so versatile and comfortable, and there are a ton of options to choose from: super high-rise leggings, compression leggings, lined leggings, jogger leggings, you name it. They're like a gentle, stretchy hug to a postpartum body, when the last thing you want is to put on a pair of jeans.

Hands-free footwear

You'll gain a new appreciation for hands-free footwear options. Whether you have a sleeping baby in your arms or in the carrier, not having to bend over to put on or take off your shoes can be a game changer. There's innovation in this space, as brands are currently releasing accessible footwear options.

Baby clothes

Comfort and safety are very important things to consider when it comes to buying clothes for your baby. Pay attention to the fabric, and opt for breathable fabrics like cotton, as babies have sensitive skin. Remember that your baby will be spending a lot of time sleeping, so keep that in mind when selecting an outfit for the day. Clothes with easily detachable decorations like sequins can be a choking hazard. Go for clothes that are easy to put on and take off. And finally, plan to stock up on larger sizes, as babies tend to grow quickly.

Laundry

Earlier in the book, I mentioned re-evaluating standards and embracing that they will likely change over time. Laundry is a great opportunity to do that. As you can probably imagine or have already experienced, with a baby comes lots of laundry. Endless laundry. Small loads, big loads, redoing the same load multiple times because you forgot it in the washing machine. That's basically your relationship with laundry for the foreseeable future. Here are a few ideas that can make your life easier when it comes to laundry.

When it comes to yourself, avoid wearing clothes that require special treatment. It's mentally hard sometimes to remember which items shouldn't go in the dryer when you're transferring a load. Wool dryer balls speed up drying time and eliminate the need for dryer sheets (one less thing to remember to buy), and you can add a few drops of essential oils to them if you want a fresh scent.

If you have a partner, you can consider divvying up tasks. One person can be in charge of doing the loads and the other in charge of putting them away. You can get different laundry bins for different colors (lights, mixed, darks) so you're at least sorting them as you're taking your clothes off, which makes one less step to do. You could also combine your laundry with the baby's to make bigger loads—just make sure you're using chemical-free detergent.

Something to consider pausing for a few years is folding your baby's clothes. Yes, in an ideal world, all the laundry would

APPAREL

be folded right as it comes out of the dryer to avoid wrinkles. But the reality is that it often doesn't happen. The sheer volume of clothes that you can go through on any given day means that even if you did manage to fold all of it, the actual amount of time it would *stay* folded is limited. If you're worried about being able to find the clothes you're looking for, it's easy to categorize the baby's clothes by dresser drawer or insert sectional compartments. One drawer for diapers, onesies, and socks. One drawer for tops, one for pants, and one for pajamas.

10

FINANCE

You might be surprised at how much your own spending habits change when you have a child, and it's important to also give yourself some grace there, as you're learning. There are so many products and services out there related to parenting and children. Some will change your life, and others will make you feel perhaps a bit silly for purchasing them, in hindsight. It's easy to end up spending a lot more than you anticipated with the arrival of a baby, no matter how much you were warned about the costs.

It can be hard to take a closer look at your finances. Financial literacy is not something that is widely taught in schools, and often personal finances are a very private thing. Decisions around money can be highly emotional. For many people, money worries are a big source of stress.

The moment I started to become more curious about my own finances, it helped a lot. I realized that I had so much more control over my situation than I initially thought. I'm sharing some of the things that I discovered along the way that truly helped me. Most of them are rooted in finding ways of cutting costs and getting the most out of money.

Monthly budget

Sitting down and making a budget is probably the single most useful thing you can do to have a better awareness of your overall financial situation, understand your spending habits, and pinpoint areas of opportunity to optimize. Download your financial statements for the past three months and calculate the average amount you spend on groceries, entertainment, clothes, home, transportation, etc. It might be a little shocking to you when you first do this step. It can be a hard realization.

Next step is determining a budget by category, using your history as a guideline. Don't worry too much about getting it right the first month that you do it. It's all about learning at this stage. Over time, you'll get better. In terms of tracking spending and reconciling with your budgeted amounts, I do this manually on an online spreadsheet. However, it you prefer a more automated approach, there are plenty of budgeting and money-saving apps out there that can help to simplify everything for you. It may take a little more time to set up, but some apps will link directly to your banking accounts, which can save you a lot of time down the road. Make sure you're using a trusted app before entering your personal banking information.

Budgeting is a great tool to avoid spending more than you're making, plan for long-term expenses, and build an emergency fund. Overall, budgeting helps to gain more financial stability, which in turn gives you more confidence to make the right decisions for your family and feel empowered to reach your goals.

Talk to your partner

Make sure to have regular communication around finances. It sounds simple and straightforward, but trust me when I say, they're not always easy conversations to have. Regardless of what maternity benefits are available to you, and whether you were working prior to having a baby or not, bringing a baby into the family means a big change to the financial picture. Depending on the nature of your partnership and the roles that you each take when it comes to money, some of the additional financial impact of the baby might weigh more heavily on one person than another, and it's important to consider this when adjusting who pays for what to avoid it becoming a contentious issue over time. Aligning on goals is the only way to work together as a team.

Negotiate

Just to be clear, I'm not asking you to haggle left and right at every chance you get. However, more things than you realize are negotiable, and if it's been a while since you've given this some thought, it could be a worthwhile exercise. Consider things like rent, credit card rates, cellphone plans, and insurance rates. Be aware of the market and options out there. Often, it doesn't hurt to inquire. If you're signing up to a new service, just asking, "Is that the best price that I can access at this time?" can have an impact. Just like asking for a raise, there's an elegant and perfectly acceptable way to do it. The first step is doing a bit of research to understand your options.

Subscriptions and services

Do a quick audit of your recurring costs, things like monthly or annual subscriptions and services. Especially things that are on automatic renewal, like apps. At minimum, it might remind you that you want to start using them again. See if maybe there are free alternatives out there that can also suit your needs.

Get a library card

If you're someone that tends to buy a lot of books, consider getting a library card. Libraries can have quite extensive collections of eBooks and audiobooks. They can also have free programs to attend with your baby and other activities.

Eat more at home

Based on the amount you spend on groceries, it's easy to calculate an average cost per meal. And while it can sometimes seem like groceries are expensive, unless you're throwing away a lot of food, the average cost per meal at home is usually way lower than in restaurants or takeaway. This can save you a lot of money each month. It made me take a more intentional approach when it came to eating in restaurants. Instead of choosing them for convenience when I was tired and out of ideas, it was more special to plan to eat out at a specific place occasionally.

Declutter your inbox

Every so often, it's a good idea to reevaluate what marketing emails you're receiving from brands, and maybe take a pause for a little bit by unsubscribing to them. It's easy to go down a rabbit hole of thinking you need new things just because a new product was released that you didn't even know you wanted.

Buy in bulk

This requires a little planning and likely a little extra space for storage, but it's a great way to save on items that you buy and consume frequently. Things like oats, flour, rice, sugar, nuts, or seeds, are very easy to buy in bulk and save. The key when comparing prices is to look at the cost per unit or gram. Over time, you can learn a good price range for frequently purchased items by heart and know right away if a sale is worth it or not.

Digital Flyers

Meal planning around sales is a great way to save without too much effort. There's a natural rotation of foods that go on sale, and often you can get good prices on produce when it's in season. As a bonus, checking flyers is a great way to get inspiration for your meal planning. You can start with the protein and decide how you want to build your meal around it from there. There are apps that aggregate all the flyers in your area and allow you to search by food item to determine the best store to purchase your groceries on any given week.

Get a savings account

If you don't have one already, I recommend opening a savings account. This can serve as a financial safety net for unexpected costs. You can also use it to plan for vacations or just reduce general financial stress. You can start small by setting up an automatic transfer of funds into your savings account every month or plan to transfer a percentage of your income every month.

Reduce energy costs

Depending on where you live, a useful method is to plan to use electricity when the rates are lower, outside of peak times, especially in the winter. You can do this by programming the dishwasher to run in the middle of the night. You can also reduce utilities costs by washing your clothes in cold water and using a drying rack when possible. You can switch all your lightbulbs to LED bulbs. These methods are all very easy to do and don't require many changes to your home. If you're renovating or updating windows, take some time to consider what your options are and if it's worth investing up front in energy-efficient or heat-efficient materials if it'll help you save down the road.

Make coffee at home

This is another way to save money, especially with the costs going up so much these days. I once calculated the difference between the cost of buying a coffee in a coffee shop versus making it at home, and the difference in cost was significant. I didn't eliminate buying lattes altogether, but it gave me a newfound appreciation for enjoying a cup at home.

Sell used items

Sell items that are no longer useful or do not bring you joy. This is a great way to declutter while also generating money in your pocket. There are many websites you can use to post your items for sale at no cost to you. Local buy and sell groups are also an option. Taking good pictures and making sure that you describe the item accurately are key to generating interest and quick sales.

Buy generic

With ever rising food costs, switching from name-brand products to generic products can have a big impact on your grocery bill. You can start with basic staples, like cleaning supplies and paper products. For some products that you've been buying for many years, at least be open to giving alternatives a try.

Subscribe and save

For some basic household items and other things like diapers, see what options exist to subscribe online to have them delivered on a regular basis. It's an easy way to save up to 5 percent, and as a bonus, it's one less thing on your list to think about and purchase.

FINANCE

Buy used

Secondhand or pre-loved items, as I like to call them, are one of my favorite ways to reduce spending, especially when you have a baby and need many new items over a short span of time. Things like clothes, toys, books, and baby gear are all things that are both easy to buy used and eventually sell as well. In fact, many bigger-ticket baby items retain their value very well and are easy to resell.

Pick one points program

The number of savings programs and points cards out there can be overwhelming. My suggestion is to do a little research and pick the one that best suits your overall needs and factors in your spending habits. In my experience, wanting to accumulate points with a particular company can sometimes lead you to make decisions that end up costing you more money. For example, by shopping at a store that doesn't have the best prices just to rack up extra points.

Simple pleasures

Sometimes we get lost in a cycle of spending more and wanting more. There are so many simple pleasures that do not cost money that we can enjoy around us. Sometimes all it takes is to be more aware of them to feel more appreciation for what these simple pleasures can give us.

Education fund

Starting this fund early is recommended, even if you're only making small contributions. It's also great as an option when your family is looking for gift ideas on birthdays or other special occasions. Sometimes there are government matching programs that make it even more worthwhile.

Backup line of credit

Outside of creating an emergency fund, consider securing a personal line of credit as an additional financial safety net for your family in case of unexpected, large costs. These often have lower interest rates than conventional credit cards and personal loans, and they generally have no minimum monthly or yearly fees.

Will or testament

This will determine what will happen to your property and assets and allow you to weigh in on who becomes your baby's guardian should they not have another parent able to care for them. You can determine exactly how they'll be provided for in terms of the finance management.

It's worth getting some advice from someone that you trust and starting the process early, because it can take longer than you'd expect, and it's important to take the time you need to have all the necessary discussions with your partner or other family members.

And while you're at it, consider getting all your other papers in order, such as creating an organized system for all your banking, insurance, and other important information, including account numbers and passwords for anybody that would need to access it, like the executor of your estate. And of course, make sure to keep this in a safe and secure location.

Learn to say no

This can be very hard at times, because you may be surrounded by other new moms in very different financial situations than you, who can afford to spend a lot on experiences and stuff for the baby. Ultimately, it's important not to feel pressured and to be able to express—without embarrassment—that a certain activity is not within your means. It can be as easy as saying, "I would love to, but that's not in my budget right now." It may take some practice.

11

WORK

While you're on maternity leave, you'll have a lot of time to reflect on and reassess how you feel about certain aspects of your life. It's valuable to take some time and think about your career while you're not working, as this will give you some perspective.

Are you inspired by your leader, or do you dread working? Do you have a mentor? What are the barriers that stand in the way of you feeling fulfilled at work? What do you think you're good at? What do you enjoy the most? When are you your best self? Now that you're a parent, does it change how you feel about your job and aspirations? Would you be open to pursing a different career that gives you more flexibility to be at home more often? Give these questions some thought.

Many people go one step further by embarking on job searches and interviewing for new roles while on maternity leave. Sometimes it's good to see what's out there and determine what is the best path for you. It might also serve to reinforce your loyalty with regards to your current position.

Depending on the length of your maternity leave, you can consider learning a new skill or taking a course that interests you. Some people yearn for additional types of stimulation in addition to caring for their baby. It doesn't need to be a big commitment; you can pick something that offers flexibility.

Some moms opt to extend their maternity leave without any paid benefits. This is a great option if you don't want to return to work and can afford not to, either temporarily or permanently. It's important to note that this can impact your employer's obligation to protect your job. However, for some, the cost of childcare can be very close to the salary that you will make, so that can be a deciding factor.

When and if you do return to work, it will be a big transition after being home with the baby. It will be harder than you expect and requires thoughtfulness. Even if you're excited to go back, you may still feel a lot of guilt when you actually do return. Here are my thoughts on how to make it as smooth as possible.

Childcare ramp-up

Try to plan a gradual introduction with your baby when it comes to childcare. You can start with a few hours and work your way up to a whole day. It's preferable to do this before you return to work so you can be close by in case things aren't going as planned or the caregiver needs additional support. This approach can also help to ease your own concerns. When you're used to spending so much time with your baby, it can be hard for you to adapt too.

Feeding plan

If you were exclusively breastfeeding the baby while on maternity leave, make a transition plan for feeding, as the baby will likely have to learn how to take a bottle for pumped milk or formula. This can be a rocky road for some and requires lots of patience.

Pumping at work

It's a necessary conversation to have with your employer if you're still nursing and need to pump milk during work hours. The discussion should include making sure that you can have breaks during the day to pump, a private place to pump that is not a restroom, access to a fridge to store your milk, and a sink to wash parts of the pump. Keep in mind that they may need a little time to prepare accommodations for you.

Gradual return

If you're very concerned about your return to work and think that a gradual start is best, talk to your employer to see if it's a possibility to work part-time for the first few weeks. This can give you the opportunity to ease into your new routine and give you extra time around childcare drop-offs and pickups. Either way, plan to start midweek on your first week to make things easier for you.

Easy dinners

Try to simplify dinners on your first week back. If you can precook some of your meals before you start, you'll only have to reheat them. See where your partner can support you during this time.

Give yourself time

Don't be too hard on yourself if you're finding that it's not going exactly as you envisioned in those first few weeks. It's normal to feel a little destabilized. It can be a very emotional time, and you may experience a lot of sadness. Try not to make any drastic decisions during this time, as it'll likely get better as you adjust. Give yourself a chance.

Expect change

No matter how long you were in your position before you left, or how short of a time you were gone, things will have changed when you get back. There will be new colleagues, new projects, new ways of doing things. You may even have a new boss. Although the thought of coming back to what you left is comforting, it's not realistic. Your job and tasks themselves might have also changed to better suit the current needs of the business.

I encourage you to have an open conversation with your manager to ensure that you're up to speed on all the changes that happened while you were gone, and that you have the clarity you need around the current expectations for your position. Avoid making assumptions, and have direct, open conversations. If your current role no longer aligns to your interests, it's worth mentioning this to see if there are any other opportunities available.

Adjust working hours

If your old hours no longer work for you now that you're a working mom, talk with your manager to see if there's any flexibility they can offer. It may not always be possible, but it's worth asking. Having a job that can be done virtually can give you lots of opportunities for alternative hours.

Be open with colleagues

Those who are not working parents may not fully comprehend all the new logistics and responsibilities that you're now facing. It's better to be upfront so they can understand, support you if needed, or facilitate changes. For example, if certain meetings at the end of the day tend to go over by thirty minutes, perhaps they can be scheduled for earlier in the day.

Know the sick policy

Now that you have a baby, you also need to factor in their sick days with your own as someone will have to care for them during this time. Children don't choose when to get sick, and the timing and frequency can be very difficult to manage on top of your work responsibilities. Get a good understanding of your employer's sick day policy. That way, you can proactively come up with solutions before you run out of options. For example, working extended hours to make up the time on other days or switching to virtual work when needed.

WORK

Workplace boundaries

The first step is to determine what they will be. It might take a bit of time to figure this piece out, but it's important. Here are a few examples. Having a cut-off time for checking work emails at night, chunks of time where you're not available because you're doing a bedtime routine with the baby, or saying no to a project because of a full workload. Workplace boundaries are especially important when you're a parent because it's very easy to fall into the trap of always prioritizing work over family.

Connect with working parents

Other working parents can help to support you. They are seasoned moms and likely have some good advice! Sometimes it's nice to be able to vent to someone that understands what you're going through and can encourage you without any judgement. If you're able to connect with colleagues, that is great. If not, there are online communities for working moms that you can find on social networks.

Outsource what you can

Going back to work means that you'll have less time to do all the things you used to do before. If it's within your financial means, there's nothing wrong with outsourcing tasks in the day-to-day management of your home so that you can reduce stress and spend more quality time with your baby. It can include hiring a cleaner, a dog walker, using a laundry service, and meal prep delivery. If you're feeling overwhelmed, you can always try it for a period to see if it helps, and take it from there.

The mommy track

This is basically the idea that becoming a mother can have an impact on your career because you'll have reduced opportunities. Even with labor standards in place, some people will act on their biases with regards to mothers when it comes to the workplace.

At the end of the day, you cannot control other people's opinions or actions. If you feel as though you haven't been treated fairly or see changes at work that don't add up, speak to your manager. Whatever you do, don't blame yourself.

What you can control, however, is how you think about yourself. The truth is, being a mother is your new superpower. You faced all sorts of new challenges and situations for which you had no experience. And you survived. Heck, you probably even thrived at times. All this on limited sleep for extended periods of time. You can have flexible hours and still have ambition *and* the same opportunities as someone without a baby. Know that there are companies that exist that support working moms and do not discriminate against them.

12

BONUS

Over the course of my two maternity leaves, I did a lot of things that my former single self would've balked at, like buying a slow cooker or getting a Costco membership and being genuinely excited about it—still am! That's the thing when you go through big life changes. You stretch and grow, and in doing so, uncover new things that you like. Maybe some things that weren't that important to you in the past are now among your biggest priorities.

I've always loved discovering new things. It feeds my natural curiosity and serves as inspiration to expand my experience of the world around me, even when it means doing something that's not in my wheelhouse. Throughout the book, I've included a few tidbits about my personal favorite things where it was relevant, but I wanted to put together an expanded collection of little extras for you. Think of this as a grab bag of ideas that may spark your interest when you're feeling stumped or too tired to think of something on your own.

USEFUL APPS

- *Waterllama*—It's what I use to track my water intake. Staying hydrated is a daily struggle, but I feel so many of the benefits when I hold myself accountable to drinking water regularly. This app has a whimsical yet super intuitive design and can track more than forty beverages. Which means you can easily see how much water you're ingesting on any given day, from milk, soup, coffee, and tea, among others.

- *Habit*—This is my go-to for tracking progress on small habits that make my life better. It's great to be able to see your own stats and get reminders if needed. I was little too ambitious at first and loaded way too many habits. I have since simplified it with only four habits that I try to do regularly. They include flossing, reading, meditating, and going out in nature. At the end of the day, when you accomplish all the daily habits that you set for yourself in the app, you get a "You did it!" message with confetti to acknowledge your efforts, which can be encouraging.

- *Headspace*—I use this app for meditation. I've tried many different mindfulness apps in the past and found that this one has the most variety and keeps me motivated to meditate. There's a video that I always start my day with called *The Wake Up*. It's only three to seven minutes long, and watching it always gives me something to reflect on. Outside of that, I'm currently doing *Headspace 365*, which is a yearlong course on the app with daily mediations. I especially like that you can skip days without penalty and continue from where you left off.

- *MinimaList*—It's a checklist and task manager app. The design is as simple as it gets. My favorite use is for my to-do list, which you can also display on a widget on your phone's lock screen, so you can easily see the top three things on your list. I also use it for my grocery list. It has other features, like alerts that you can program, but I've kept it simple.

AUTHORS I LOVE

- Emily Oster is an economics professor at Brown University and the author of the book that resonated so much with me during my pregnancy, called *Expecting*

Better. Emily's also written other books on parenting, *Cribsheet* and *The Family Firm*. In her books, she looks at the data relating to pregnancy and parenting with the aim of helping readers with decision-making.

- Oliver Jeffers is a visual artist, author, and a great storyteller. His children's books are the ones that I keep going back to, over and over, notably *The Fate of Fausto*, *What We'll Build*, *There's a Ghost in This House*, and *The Moose Belongs to Me*.

- Jeannette Walls is a writer and journalist. Her memoir about her childhood and dysfunctional family, *The Glass Castle*, remains one of my all-time favorite books. I also loved her first novel, *Half Broke Horses: A True-Life Novel*. She has this way of pulling you into a whole other world, which I very much enjoy.

BOOKS TO READ

- *The Boy, the Mole, the Fox and the Horse* by Charlie Mackesy, an illustrated book for all ages.
- *Neapolitan Novels* by Elena Ferrante, a four-part series of fiction about friendship and coming of age.
- *The Happy Sleeper* by Heather Turgeon and Julie Wright, a research-based guide to help children sleep.
- *Hunt, Gather, Parent* by Michaeleen Doucleff, lessons from ancient cultures to raise happy children.

- *Milk and Honey* by Rupi Kaur, a collection of poetry on survival, feminism, and relationships.

MUSIC TO DISCOVER

- *murmures* by Jean-Michel Blais
- *Foule sentimentale* by Chilly Gonzales
- *Lost River* by Cœur de pirate
- *Holm Sound* by Erland Cooper
- *Dreams* by Sergio Díaz de Rojas
- *Motion* by Peter Sandberg

SHOWS TO WATCH

- *Fleabag,* a comedy-drama starring Phoebe Waller-Bridge.
- *Bad Sisters,* a dark comedy starring Sharon Horgan.
- *The OA,* a sci-fi mystery-drama starring Brit Marling.
- *Catastrophe,* a transatlantic romance starring Sharon Hogan and Rob Delaney.
- *Insecure,* a comedy series featuring the friendship of two women, starring Issa Rae.
- *Starstruck,* a comedy sitcom starring Rose Matafeo.

INSTAGRAM HANDLES TO CHECK OUT

- Dr. Becky Kennedy is a psychologist, mother, and founder of Good Inside. She offers practical strategies for parents to better understand their child's behavior and help strengthen their connections. There are many additional ways to access her content, such as a community-powered membership with trained coaches, a podcast, and a book. The reason I like her Instagram is because the content is presented in a very digestible format on a platform that I frequent regularly. Her short, relatable videos on specific parenting challenges include easy ways to put her advice into action right away. Sometimes I'm not even in the mindset of improving my parenting skills, but then I stumble across one of her videos and feel inspired to try a new strategy. It also feels comforting to know that I'm not alone with the struggles I'm facing. *@drbeckyatgoodinside*

- Care Sinclair is a busy mom of four, as well as being a registered midwife, CPR instructor, certified car seat technician, babywearing educator, and infant mental health specialist. In her words, she offers family-focused education and support for expectant and young families. She is also a content creator and hosts classes and workshops. It's hard to express the extent of the positive impact she had on me during mat leave. She has this gentle yet firm way of making motherhood less daunting. Helps you gain the knowledge you need to make the best choices for your family without compromising safety. *@with_care*

BONUS

- Nedra Glover Tawwab is a therapist, mother, and author. Her area of expertise is relationships and boundaries. From the moment I discovered her online, I gravitated to her content because it's straightforward and extremely helpful. She puts together these lists on things to consider and say when you're being challenged, or things that can happen in certain circumstances. She also has great videos with a very calm but firm voice of reason. Being exposed to her insight regarding a multitude of situations always leaves me with a tremendous feeling of empowerment and gives me so much clarity about my own life and how to make it better. *@nedratawwab*

- Dr. Rachel Schwartzman is a naturopathic doctor, mother, and birth doula. She offers great advice on a variety of topics relating to health and well-being. What I enjoy the most, however, is the plant-based food content that she posts, like salads, bowls, soups, crumbles, cookies, and loafs. Sometimes it's an easy recipe, such as her classic date squares. Other times she just shares whatever she's making for dinner that night, along with the ingredients and instructions needed to replicate it. She also includes when the food is kid approved, which is always helpful. My all-time favorite recipe of hers—that I made countless times while on maternity leave—is for raw, vegan energy balls. *@rachels_nd*

MOST PRIZED COOKBOOKS

- *Small Victories* by Julia Turshen. This cookbook was recommended to me by a dear friend during my first maternity leave, and it's safe to say that I've cooked my way through almost every dish since. With more than four hundred easy recipes, it was a cookbook that I always kept close to me. The one meal that I make regularly to this day is her Roasted Salmon with Maple and Soy. I stopped buying salad dressing when I discovered her No-Sweat Vinaigrette. Other favorites include the Potluck Quinoa and the Sour Cream Pancakes with Roasted Blueberries.

- *It's All Good* by Gwyneth Paltrow and Julia Turshen. It was Julia Turshen that first drew me to this book, as I was such a big fan of hers, and it soon became a favorite because of all of the healthy yet delicious recipes using wholesome food found within. It also expanded my repertoire of ingredients. Favorite recipes include the Spanish Style Barbecued Chicken, Sautéed Corn with Chimichurri, Roasted Cauliflower and Chickpeas with Mustard and Parsley, and the Mexican Green Goddess Dressing.

BONUS

- *Slower is Better* and *Slow Cooker Favorites* by Ricardo Larrivée. These are the two books that solidified my interest in slow cooking and kept me coming back to try new dishes. There are such a wide variety of recipes, you might end up eating slow cooker meals every night of the week for a little while. Maybe I overdid it, but let's just say I was enthusiastic. The recipe for making chicken stock is now my go-to. One thing that I found particularly useful was that it noted whenever a recipe would freeze well. This was very practical information to have when making larger quantities of food with the goal of saving a portion for a future dinner.

- *Make Every Dish Delicious* by Leslie Chesterman. It's a more comprehensive cookbook in that it has tips on how to set up your kitchen, with dishes for so many occasions, including modern classics. This is a newer book to my collection, but I have loved everything I have tried thus far and am very eager to cook my way through. I'm particularly excited to try all the recipes within her Feast of Choice section on Thanksgiving. I also plan on taking her advice regarding getting family members to help so that you're not the only one cooking.

FOODS TO TRY

- *Dates*—They were an acquired taste for me, after seeing my mother enjoy them for years without much interest on my part to try them. I have, however, made up for lost time, because for the last several years, I have eaten at least one a day. Medjool dates are typically easy to find and very delicious, but other types of dates work just as well. Usually, I grab a spoonful of peanut butter and stick a date in it—it's super yummy. I have expanded to try other combinations, like dates and dark chocolate or dates and mascarpone. One that I have yet to try but am looking forward to is dates and marzipan. I don't usually have marzipan on hand, which reminds me that I should do something about that!

- *Irish soda bread*—It's easy to make at home and does not require yeast, which is a great time-saver. It took me a little while to fully appreciate it, as it's quite dense. But over time, I've come to crave it much more than other types of bread. I was introduced to it by my mother, and this is her recipe. It's the only version I've ever tried, and it's hard to mess up. I usually slice the whole loaf and freeze it for easy access for toast and to maintain freshness.

BONUS

2 cups whole wheat flour

½ tsp kosher salt

1 tsp baking soda

1 tsp baking powder

1 egg beaten

1 cup full-fat plain yogurt

1 tbsp maple syrup or honey

Instructions

Preheat oven to 375°F. Mix wet ingredients in one bowl. Dry ingredients in another. Combine the two. Knead a bit. Add some flour if needed. Grease a loaf pan with olive oil. Add the dough and cut a few slits, about one-half-inch deep, diagonally, to allow bread to rise. Bake for about thirty-five to forty minutes until golden brown. Let stand for ten minutes. Hot tip: it's delicious with some butter while it's still warm.

Variations

Instead of a loaf pan, you can use a baking sheet with parchment paper. Buttermilk can be used instead of yogurt, though you may have to adjust the flour a bit. If you prefer unbleached flour, you can substitute that for the whole wheat flour. Consider adding mix-ins like seeds, nuts, raisins, or currants, or sesame seeds on top.

- *Molasses*—Another thing that I always have stocked in my pantry and eat every day. If you're not familiar with it, it's a dark, sweet, and thick syrup that's used as an ingredient in things like gingerbread cookies. I usually have regular molasses on toast (you can use Irish soda bread!) mixed with peanut butter. It may sound a little unusual, but the flavors of the peanut butter and molasses really balance each other out. Blackstrap molasses, which is typically less sweet and has a higher concentration of vitamins and minerals, is great for baking.

- *Yogurt, chia seeds, and wheat germ*—This is what I eat for breakfast every day. One cup of full-fat plain yogurt, cover the top with a generous amount of chia seeds (like 1–2 tbsp) and sprinkle everything with some toasted wheat germ (you can buy it toasted). Stir it well with a spoon, and then let it sit for a few minutes, enough for the chia seeds to expand a little. But don't leave it too long, or it'll be too thick. And then enjoy! I mainly eat the yogurt for the probiotics that can help with gut health. The chia seeds are a great source of fiber. The wheat germ is to add some grains and other essential nutrients. Part of the reason I like this breakfast is because it's fast to make, easy to keep the ingredients on hand, and you can eat it with one hand. Having the same breakfast every day also takes stress away from deciding what to eat, and that's a good thing when you're preoccupied with baby's breakfast!

- *Pâté chinois*—It's a well-known dish from Quebec, where I was born and raised. It resembles shepherd's pie or cottage pie, but it has distinct ingredients. Basically, it's a casserole with cooked ground beef at the bottom, a middle layer of corn (canned or creamed, or a mixture of both), followed by mashed potatoes on top. Sprinkling paprika is also a must as final touch, and it's preferably eaten with ketchup. You know when someone asks you what meal you would choose to eat for the rest of your life if you were stranded on an island? This would be my choice, as it's the perfect comfort food. Babies usually love it too.

- *Green juice*—I mentioned earlier in the book that instead of making fresh green juice every day, I now make big batches of green juice, enough to last two weeks, which I freeze into individual daily portions. My preference is a centrifugal juicer over a masticating juicer. Although they're less effective at extracting juice, they're faster and less expensive. I recommend choosing one with a large feed chute to reduce prep time (e.g., large enough to take whole apples) and with a juice container that has a large capacity (at least sixty ounces). Fresh juice from a centrifugal juicer is good for up to twenty-four hours in the fridge and at least six months in the freezer.

When you want to drink it, you can defrost it by placing it in the fridge the day before. If you want to consume it on the same day, you can place the container with frozen juice in a bowl of cold water on the counter for a little while. Once defrosted, you can drink it as is, but it tastes better as a base for a green smoothie. I blend it with other ingredients, such as banana, avocado, spirulina, and wheatgrass. You can add other things like dates, nut butter, and spinach. Here's my big batch green juice recipe that I have perfected over the last few years:

1–2 lbs. spinach
1 bunch of green kale (leafy parts only)
2–3 heads of romaine lettuce
4 limes peeled, white pith on
4–6 zucchinis (stem cut off)
8 large cucumbers
1 bunch of celery (stalks only)
6 gala apples (no need to core)
1 fennel bulb (end cut off)

BONUS

Instructions

Make sure to wash all produce thoroughly. Organic is preferable but not mandatory. It's nice to have a fresh glass of green juice the day you make it, with a little ice if you like it cold. When juicing, the order of ingredients is important, to avoid clogging the small holes in the filter and diminishing its efficiency. Start with leafy greens, then soft fruits, and end with the harder vegetables and fruits. You need to plan to have a large bowl to transfer the juice a few times from the juice container as you make it, since this recipe will yield quite a lot of juice. It's important to stir the juice well before dividing into smaller portions for freezing.

Variations

Feel free to add cameo ingredients or make substitutions to add a variety of the vitamins and nutrients to your juice. Some vegetables can have a significant impact on the flavor and color (and not always in a good way!), so keep that in mind when introducing something new, and always start with a small quantity. You can consider adding things like yellow bell peppers, parsley, mint, or ginger. Limes can be replaced with lemons. Apples can be replaced with pears or some pineapple.

A few final thoughts on juicing... If you've never had green juice before, you probably won't love it instantly, unless you have a natural penchant for all things green. It takes a little time for your palate to adjust and to feel the benefits in your body. In my case, I've seen improvements with digestion, the softness of my skin, and my levels of energy. I've also seen an impact on my mind and mental well-being, as I have more cognitive clarity when I add green juice to my daily food intake. All this to say, if drinking green juice is new for you, I recommend that you give it a little time to determine if it's something you want to keep doing.

CONCLUSION

No matter how long or short your maternity leave is, you'll likely feel at some point that you didn't have as much control over it as you would've liked. This is normal. When it comes to your baby, no amount of wishing for something can guarantee that it'll happen. This is a lesson I've carried with me into other aspects of life.

Embrace the chaos, and when things are hard, remember that each phase will eventually run its course. If you're spending too much time unhappy or wishing things were different, talk to someone about it. Complex and lesser-known emotions during this time are very common and treatable. They should not lead you to feel isolated. Seek maternal health support if needed.

Parental challenges are an intrinsic part of the experience. Trusting your internal compass will help you navigate them. Don't overwhelm yourself with a misguided ideal of being the perfect self-sufficient parent. Yes, asking for help is not easy. And if you do get support from your community and family, in your own time, acknowledge it. Don't ever forget that you get to decide what's best for your baby, and you don't have to compromise your core beliefs.

Remember to balance the needs of your baby with your own needs. This won't always be possible, and that's okay. Just don't forget about YOU in all this. Sometimes it's necessary to hit pause for a second. Literally. If you're watching a movie, just pause it. Look around. Zone into the sound of crickets chirping or look out the window and try to find the moon. When all else fails, just close your eyes for two minutes. Put a timer on your phone.

You'll find that you're stronger than you ever thought possible. Breathe. Stop trying to micromanage everything. Learn to surrender and let go. Not everything can be planned or prevented. Say no when you have to. Some days, you'll feel like a bad mom. Other days, you'll feel invincible. Try to practice self-empathy no matter what you're facing. You won't get it right all the time. Motherhood is not a competitive sport. Once in a while, look over your shoulder to see how far you have come.

And remember, all things grow with love.

ABOUT THE AUTHOR

Emily Malloy was born in Montréal, Quebec. She graduated from McGill University with a degree in Economics. She is an executive with over 15 years of experience in the advertising industry. Her innovative work has been recognized through numerous awards in the span of her career. She is also a mentor, helping young marketers achieve professional success. She lives in Toronto, Ontario, with her two children and spends her free time in her home in the Laurentians, Quebec.

www.EmilyMalloy.ca
_emily_malloy

Made in the USA
Middletown, DE
27 August 2023